TEACHING SECONDARY ENGLISH

General Editor: Peter King

ENCOURAGING WRITING

ENCOURAGING WRITING

ROBERT PROTHEROUGH

London   METHUEN   *New York*

First published in 1983 by
Methuen & Co. Ltd
11 New Fetter Lane, London EC4P 4EE
Published in the USA by
Methuen & Co.
in association with Methuen, Inc.
733 Third Avenue, New York, NY 10017

© *1983 Robert Protherough*

Phototypeset by
Tradespools Limited, Frome, Somerset
Printed in Great Britain by
Richard Clay (The Chaucer Press)
Bungay, Suffolk

British Library Cataloguing in Publication
Data

Protherough, Robert
  Encouraging writing.—(Teaching
Secondary English series)
  1. Creative writing (Secondary
education)
  2. English language—Study and
teaching—Great Britain
  I. Title   II. Series
  808'.042   LB1631

  ISBN 0-416-34050-4
  ISBN 0-416-34060-1 Pbk

Library of Congress Cataloguing in
Publication Data

Protherough, Robert.
  Encouraging writing.
  (Teaching Secondary English series)
  Bibliography: p.
  Includes index.
  1. English language—Composition and
exercises—Study and teaching.
  2. Language arts. I. Title. II. Series.
  PE1404.P7 1983   808'.042'071
  83-12086

  ISBN 0-416-34050-4
  ISBN 0-416-34060-1 (pbk.)

CONTENTS

GENERAL EDITOR'S PREFACE

English remains a core subject in the secondary school curriculum as the confident words of a recent HMI document reveal:—

> English is of vital importance in the development of pupils as individuals and as members of society: our language is our principal means of making sense of our experience and communication with others. The teaching of English is concerned with the essential skills of speech, reading and writing, and with literature. Schools will doubtless continue to give them high priority.
>
> (*The School Curriculum*, DES, 1981)

Such confidence belies the fact that there has been, and continues to be, much debate among practitioners as to exactly what constitutes English. If the desired consensus remains rather far off at least the interested teacher now has a large and useful literature on which he or she can profitably reflect in the attempt to answer the question 'What is English?' There have been notable books designed to reorientate teachers' thinking about the subject ranging from those absorbed by the necessary theoretical analysis, like John Dixon's *Growth Through English* (Oxford, rev. edn 1975), to those working outwards from new research into classroom language, like *From Communication to Curriculum*, by Douglas Barnes (Penguin, 1976); but there are not so many books intended to help teachers get a purchase on their day-to-day activities (a fine exception is *The English Department Handbook* recently published by the ILEA English Centre). To gain such a purchase requires confidence built not from making 'everything new' so much as learning to combine the best from the older traditions with some of those newer ideas. And preferably these ideas have to be seen to have emerged from effective classroom teaching. The English teacher's aims have to be continually reworked in the light of new experience, and the assurance necessary to manage this is bred out of the convictions of other experienced practitioners. This is of particular importance to the new and inexperienced teacher. It is to such teachers and student teachers that this series is primarily directed.

The books in this series are intended to give practical guidance in the various areas of the English curriculum. Each area is treated in a separate volume in order to gain the necessary space in which to discuss it at some length. The aim of the series is twofold: to describe good practice by exploring the approaches and activities reflected in the daily work of an English teacher in the comprehensive school; and to give a practical lead to teachers who wish to try out for themselves a wider repertoire of teaching skills and ways of organizing syllabuses and lessons. Taken as a whole, the series does not press upon the reader a ready-made philosophy, but attempts to provide a map of the English teaching landscape in which the separate volumes highlight an individual feature of that terrain, representing its particular characteristics while reminding us of the continuity between these differing elements in the overall topography.

The series addresses itself to the 11–16 age range with an additional volume on sixth-form work, and assumes a mixed ability grouping, at least in the first two years of schooling. Each volume begins with a discussion of the problems and rationale of its chosen aspect of English and goes on to describe practical ways in which the teachers can organize their syllabus and lessons to achieve their intended goals, and ends with a brief guide to books, resources, etc. The individual volumes are written by experienced teachers with a particular interest in their chosen area and the ideas they express have been proved by them or their colleagues in their own classrooms.

It is at the level of the practical that any synthesis of the various approaches to English can be gained, and to accomplish this every teacher must be in possession of a rationale and an awareness of good methods wherever and however they have been achieved. By reading the books in this series it is to be hoped that teachers will be encouraged to try out for themselves ideas found effective by their colleagues so gaining the confidence to make their own informed choice and planning in their own classrooms.

Peter King
July 1983

ACKNOWLEDGEMENTS

Teachers are learning continually, not least from those they teach. There are few really original ideas about writing or the teaching of it, and most of us find it impossible to remember where our principles and practices originally came from. We develop them from colleagues, who had adapted them from others, who themselves took them from a book or lecture in the first place. That is how it is with teaching.

My thanks have to be very wide ones, then. I am grateful to the many children in different schools with and through whom I have developed my ideas, to colleagues who talked things over with me, to graduate students whose lessons I have watched and learned from, to teachers who have shared insights on in-service courses, and to many friends in the National Association for the Teaching of English. Those teachers and authors whose help can be specifically identified are acknowledged in the references to the following chapters. I owe a particular debt, though, to Judith Atkinson, Head of English first at Sydney Smith Senior High School and more recently at Wolfreton School, who has allowed me to work with her pupils, has provided much of the school material quoted in this book, and has read the manuscript with a professional eye.

The final text owes much to my wife, Margaret, not least for her typing of early drafts which eliminated many errors and infelicities. I must also thank Mrs Nicky Hamlett for her expert typing of the final version. I am especially grateful to Peter King, the general editor of this series, for his continuing encouragement, his perceptive criticisms of early drafts and a number of helpful suggestions. The surviving errors, like the opinions expressed here, are the responsibility of the author.

PART ONE:
RATIONALE

Introduction

When I went into school I had twenty-four good ideas for getting kids to write but no real ideas about what to do with the writing once I'd got it.

It was easy to pick out the few really good or really poor compositions in each set, but most of them couldn't be distinguished from each other.

Most of the writing activities went well, some not so well, but it was pretty random. There was no real programme of writing in the school; they were all one-off lessons.

Comments like these, made by students looking back over a term's teaching practice in secondary schools, reveal some of the aspects of writing in school that baffle them – and most of us. They are conscious of having only a hazy awareness (the significantly repeated phrase is 'no real idea') of the purposes of writing, of what their teaching is supposed to achieve, of how it should be organized, or of how they should respond to children's work. This is not to blame the students (or even their tutor!). Their minds are inevitably fixed on the class that they are going to have to face. Encouraged, perhaps, by notions of creative writing that see the teacher as providing 'stimulus' or 'triggering' response, students concentrate on finding those apparently infallible 'good ideas for getting kids to write'. Such an activity seems to them eminently 'practical'. Only with experience do they learn that knowledge of what is involved in the writing process, some sense of development in writing, or the ability to assess writing coherently and consistently are equally 'practical'. Indeed, lesson ideas can only be rationally chosen within the framework of this knowledge.

Before dealing with the planning and organizing of the writing programme in the classroom, therefore, this volume begins with the rationale for what follows. These pages briefly introduce some of the issues which teachers need to consider, and about which they have to make their own decisions.

1
THREE BASIC QUESTIONS

Why write?

Learning to write is one of the few school activities which students rate as highly in importance as their teachers do. In a recent Hull enquiry, virtually all second- and third-year pupils across the ability range said that they thought it was 'very important'. Their reasons for making this judgement show how far they have assimilated their parents' and teachers' views of the structure of society. They know that they will be assessed – as students, as employees, and perhaps even as people – primarily by the way they write. Most of their answers to the question 'Why write?' fall into two functional categories.

The first and predictably the most common group of reasons concerns life beyond school: writing is important because it will gain you qualifications and enable you to obtain and succeed at a job at an appropriate level. Second-year pupils said, for example,

You have to write for an interview for a job when you leave school.

If you get a job as an accountant, solicitor or secretary, you need to be able to write, as in many other jobs.

How can you get a job as a secretary or librarian if you cannot write?

Even a policeman or policewoman need to be good at writing for doing their everyday reports.

The sequences and emphases of these 12-year-olds (accountants and solicitors take priority over secretaries; '*even* a policeman ...') indicate their underlying sense of social status as being somewhat linked to the level of writing ability. This awareness of being classified comes out even more markedly in the comments of third-year students:

When you leave school if you are a thoughtful writer you will probably be thought of as an intelligent person.

An illiterate person does not get on far in life, and also many people think it is a sign of stupidity.

These students were also aware that their social and personal lives were likely to demand writing. They mentioned explicitly letters, messages, diaries, notes, complaints, enquiries and keeping records. One third-year girl remarked with resignation, 'Even if you don't work you have to be able to write letters etc so there is no escape from needing to write well.' Once again there was an underlying sense of social judgement. As one second-year boy recorded ruefully, 'If you write a leter and it has a lot of speling mestakes in it you get very embarrast.'

The second most common cluster of reasons concerned the nature of school learning, and the extent to which writing is the dominant mode in which education is carried on. One third-year girl said, 'Learning to write is the most important part of school work.'

Learning to write is very important because nearly everything you do in school you write about.

Writing in school shows how much you have learnt and understood.

If you can't write you can't keep notes and therefore lose all your work and other parts of a subject which are vital to remember.

There is some uncertainty whether the importance of the writing is primarily for the pupil or for the teacher. With brutal directness, one 12-year-old girl said, 'If you did not write, the teacher could not be sure you have done your work.' They know that members of staff – particularly in English – will themselves be judged primarily by the success which their pupils show in written examinations. From the teacher's point of view, the great importance of writing is that, unlike talk which evaporates, writing lasts. It is a form which can easily be corrected, restructured and revised; comparisons can be made; language forms can be analysed. Pupils can be made more conscious of precisely what they want to express; they can look back and monitor what they are producing; their work can be made available to wider audiences. In these senses writing *is* a vital mode of learning. Indeed, Janet Emig has argued, drawing on contemporary psychologists, that it is not merely valuable but unique.

> Writing serves learning uniquely because writing as process-and-product possesses a cluster of attributes that correspond uniquely to certain powerful learning strategies.... higher cognitive functions, such as analysis and synthesis, seem to develop most fully only with the support system of verbal language – particularly, it seems, of written language.[1]

Few students saw writing as important for less directly functional reasons: for what it did to *them*, for the pleasure they gained from it, or for the possibility of expressing their own feelings and ideas. This echoed the research of the Schools Council's *Arts and the Adolescent* project, which found that 'English was given an unmistakably non-arts, non-creative 'academic' profile by the pupils'.[2] Here is a crucial difference. Teachers and students both see learning to write as extremely important, but for quite different reasons. Surveys of English teachers suggest that they attribute value to writing particularly because it is a satisfying and liberating means of self-expression and self-discovery, one that helps us to find out what we know and how we feel. Policy statements talk of the pleasure of 'making' in words, the encouragement of personal development, the ability to detach oneself from experience and to examine it, the power to share insights with a wider range of people, developing imagination and creativity, being able to 'try on' stances and opinions, and exploring situations from other people's viewpoints.

Why don't the students share these views? The nearest they get to them are occasional remarks like 'As you learn to write well, you can express your own ideas and feelings properly' or 'Writing helps you to gain a more mature way of expressing yourself'. It may be that they are suspicious of what might seem pretentious justifications, or that the concepts involved are too advanced for them to express. On the other hand, it may simply be that their teachers have never convinced them about what writing can do. Are we failing to make out the case for writing as self-expression, either because the work we are doing with them is inappropriate or because our own attitudes show that we don't really believe it?

To sum up, then, it seems encouraging that pupils and teachers share opinions about the importance of learning to write. At a more profound level, though, it could be seen as disturbing that so few pupils express views of writing as meeting their *own* immediate needs. The great majority ventriloquially speak the opinions of parents and teachers: children must learn to write because they will need that ability as working adults or in order to succeed at school. Such views give some support to those critics who fear that learning to write can be seen as a repressive instrument of social control.

Why is there resistance?

There seems to be a natural drive in young children to write: they leave their early scribblings everywhere, on the wall-paper, in printed books, on steamed-up windows, on any available scrap of paper, in chalk on pavements and walls. Those who study children's unofficial writing are struck by the sheer amount of it, and by the fact that virtually all children do it. One research study concluded that, 'In almost any setting, children's unassigned writing exceeds their writing on assigned topics.'[3] It seems a reasonable hypothesis that writing is a natural, enjoyable activity, like painting, singing or dancing, until something happens to inhibit this form of expression. There is evidence that pupils in secondary school view writing less favourably than they did in the primary stage,[4] though even at the age of 15 only one pupil out of forty expresses 'a total dislike of writing'.[5] Why is it that a minority of children lose the urge to write? If – as suggested in the last section – writing is seen as so important, then why are some of them reluctant to embark on it?

When they complain, 'I can't think of anything to write about' or 'I've got nothing to say', we may attribute this to a general discontent with the school situation, or to their laziness, or to the inappropriateness of the assignment we set, or to a suspicion that they have nothing to say to us as audience. Underlying all of these, however, is almost certainly a set of assumptions about writing, established by their experiences of schooling. To have 'nothing to say' can usually be translated:

> Writing is a meaningless chore to be undertaken for the teacher's benefit not for mine, and therefore to be avoided if possible.

> *or* When I write, I make a lot of mistakes which have to be laboriously corrected, I get bad marks and I feel a failure.

or Writing demands special qualities like imagination or
creativity and I don't have them.

What is more, for every child who openly protests at having
to write there are probably five who simply resort to a kind of
passive resistance. They write as briefly as possible, revealing
little of themselves and their feelings, concentrating on
avoiding errors by using simple constructions and words of
whose spelling they are confident. The consequent writing is
dead and inert. Andrew Wilkinson has presented graphic
instances of this[6] in the work of middle-school children who,
when talking about their holiday experiences, use language in
a lively, spontaneous, personal way, but when asked to write
on the same topic, produce work like this:

> We went to pisa. We all had an ice-cream. It was a very hot
> day. I had a chocolate one, then we went to the tower I was
> the first one to the top. Pisa is a very small town.

It is not hard to think of reasons why writing may have
unattractive associations for children who are resistant in
either of these two ways.

For example:

  i) As compared with speech, writing deprives the child of
      immediate feedback, seems an artificial rather than a
      natural activity, demands greater explicitness and preci-
      sion and involves the physical difficulty of manipulating
      pen on paper. Writing is slow and hard, compared with
      talking. Indeed, learning to avoid writing may often seem
      less trouble than actually doing it.
 ii) School writing is linked with discipline in the punitive
      sense. Student-teachers with difficult classes are advised
      to give them plenty of writing to keep them in order.
      Punishments are still not uncommonly given in the form
      of writing: mechanical copying of lines, or composition
      of so many pages.

iii) Writing embodies an enduring record of mistakes, mis-understandings and embarrassing failures. The exercise book, with its trail of red ink, is a constant reminder of lack of success. The past cannot be wiped out in the way that spoken errors can be forgotten. Writing difficulties can be linked to the individual's self-image. Tony can talk freely but avoids writing because it makes him seem 'intellectually inferior'.[7]

iv) Other issues, particularly the quality of handwriting, neatness and layout, tend to be confused with the ability to write in the sense of composing. Whatever the actual intentions of the teachers, many children still perceive their real concern as being with accuracy rather than with content. One survey of attitudes found that young children of all ability levels, asked how their teachers decided what was a good piece of writing, most commonly responded with these criteria: 'It has to be long, not be messy, and have no mistakes.'[8] Parents not infrequently reinforce this idea by checking their children's books to see whether all errors have been marked.

v) The attitudes of adults rub off. Many parents have unpleasant memories of being forced to write in school, and their expectations of difficulty and failure may carry over to their children. Most students rarely see adults writing, and almost never see them doing it for pleasure. They will see their teachers enjoying talking and reading, and this modelling is an important influence on their own practice. Only rarely will they encounter such models of teachers' writing. An American survey suggests that teachers 'do not write because they don't like writing, feel they are poor writers, do not have time to write because of teaching demands, or do not believe it necessary to practise writing in order to teach it'.[9]

vi) Particularly in the fourth and fifth years, the written tasks given are perceived as uniformly dull. There is a striking correspondence between the comments of the Inspectorate in the secondary survey and those of the Assessment of Performance Unit (APU) in their survey of the language of 15-year-olds. The HMIs described the 'general uniformity of demand', which meant that notes, exercises and formal essays could amount to 200,000 words of writing in six subjects over four terms.

> The pattern most frequently found could be described as essentially one of 'notes' and 'essays', interspersed with the practice of answering examination questions alongside the drills of exercises and tests. This pattern did not make it easy for pupils to feel that their individual reactions were valued, or that their variations of information or opinion were welcome. Their files at times demonstrated the successful imprinting of a standard language, arising from teacher or textbook.[10]

In considering students' attitudes, the APU concluded that 'when dislikes in writing were analysed, pupils' answers strikingly conformed: a combined total of 60 per cent of the sample expressed a dislike for essays, copying notes, written exercises and comprehensive work'.[11]

How does the English teacher try to overcome negative reactions to writing? How do you change false assumptions? Briefly, a child with 'nothing to say' has probably not had enough encouragement to unlock that store of inner experience which we all of us build up at first hand from our daily lives and at second hand from all that we hear and read and see. Children have within themselves the essential subject matter they require. What they may lack is confidence, assurance of interest and appropriate practice. Overcoming resistance may involve, for instance:

  i) encouraging the sharing of anecdotes and recollections – in talk at first – to build up assurance that the child's experiences are of interest;

ii) providing a wide range of visual and aural source material and diagnosing what seems to 'tap into' the child's inner speech;

iii) encouraging writing for real audiences and for specific purposes that are made clear from the beginning;

iv) organizing group work in which the child is placed with enthusiastic writers;

v) demonstrating that the teacher reads as a sympathetic and encouraging helper, interested in what is being read, not primarily as an error-detector or mark-giver.

One difficulty, however, is that as teachers we also have our own hang-ups and false assumptions about writing, and the teaching of writing. Chapter 2 offers an opportunity to consider what our own attitudes are, and how these are likely to affect our classroom practice.

Can writing be taught?

When I was at secondary school in the 1940s, I was given a weekly topic for composition ('The autobiography of a pair of boots', I remember, and 'Honesty is the best policy'), to be written in my own time, and later to be returned to me with errors indicated and a mark or grade at the bottom. Was I being taught to write? Certainly my writing improved, but did teaching have much to do with it? Was it simply the opportunity for practice, increasing maturity and an innate responsiveness to what I was reading? (It's all too clear where the influence of Leacock and Wodehouse on my style gave place to Saki and Oscar Wilde.) The methods being practised with me were grounded in a particularly English cynicism about intervening in such a mysterious process. Sixty years ago George Sampson said that opinion 'oscillates between these two extremes, first ... that any one can write without special teaching, and next, a belief that no one can be taught to write by any quantity of teaching. Neither belief is sound'.[12]

Many of the assumptions that went with such a view, and with the associated teaching methods, live on today:

i) The emphasis is on the written product, not on the way in which it is produced.

ii) The reception concentrates on the accuracy of usage (spelling, punctuation and syntax) and the acceptability of style.

iii) The task is arbitrary and the title alone is supposed to define form, tone, mode and audience. It is largely isolated from other work being done in school and from the actual experience of the writer.

iv) Writing is seen as a private matter, to be carried out in isolation.

v) This stress on privacy and the assumption of the uniqueness of the creative act lead to the repudiation of any real attempt to teach the writing process itself, except for proof-reading and editing.

Such assumptions are so deep-rooted that children themselves see 'learning to write' in these terms, even when they are being taught in a more enlightened and understanding way. When representative groups of children aged 12–14 were asked whether they thought their writing had improved during the last school year, only one in ten thought there had been no real change for the better. When they were asked what was involved in learning to write better, though, and in what respects they still hoped to improve, their unprompted responses made it clear that the mechanics of language bulked most largely for them. Extension of vocabulary and better spelling were mentioned by about 60 per cent of them, followed by more accurate grammar and punctuation. By comparison, abilities in handling language for particular purposes were much less mentioned: descriptive or narrative ability by about one in seven, power to convey ideas or feelings by one in ten, improved style or technique by under 5 per cent. A few pupils thought that the marks of better writing were greater length, quicker speed or neater work. Some of them were interestingly aware that changes in writing were related to changes in the writer: that both had become more 'mature' or 'professional', more 'creative' or 'imaginative', or simply more 'involved' and 'enthusiastic'.

The arguments which periodically enliven the educational press about whether or not writing can be taught ('A skill which can't be taught', 'Subject of scandal', 'Creative writing – is it as bad as all that?', 'Why the kipper-sniffers are all at sea' proclaim the headlines)[13] originate largely in confusions of terminology. However boringly obvious it may seem, it is necessary to distinguish between the different though overlapping meanings we can attach to that phrase 'learning to write':

i) Handling the written mode, learning orthography ('I can do joined-up writing').

ii) Using written language without major errors in spelling, grammar and punctuation.

iii) Employing writing effectively to achieve different purposes (science notes, history essays, letters to friends).

iv) Developing the ability to produce a literary work (poem, story, play) that will give pleasure to an audience.

v) Training to become a professional writer.

It is also obvious that teaching becomes progressively less significant and less simple as we move from each of these functions to the next. The emphasis of this book is on meanings *iii* and *iv* above, for which the term *composing* – now becoming common in America – might be clearer.

Our classroom methods imply and transmit views of how writing ability is acquired. Those who taught me clearly believed that regular practice was enough: you learn the rules of the game as you go along. At the same time, others were being drilled in formal Latinate grammar on the mistaken assumption that their writing would be improved by this, that there would be a transfer between knowing about structures and being able to use them effectively. Others were more sensibly encouraged to read a great deal, in the belief that there would be a carrying-over from what is read to what is written. These underlying assumptions were rarely voiced or examined; they rested on faith rather than on evidence.

Evidence is hard to come by, of course, because there are too many variables. What happens in children as they are learning to write can never be fully known – nor can what happens as we teach. The process cannot be broken down into neat steps, like making jam tarts or mending a puncture. At what point does 'composing' begin, and where does it end? Indeed, is there one composing process, or do different written outcomes demand different acts of composing? What is the place of invention in the process? Is it true – as sometimes seems to be suggested – that you can teach writing in certain modes (how to compose a business letter or a formal report) but not others (a poem, say)? If so, then what is the reason?

Perhaps instead of asking 'Can writing be taught?' we should be asking 'Can teachers help children to become writers?'. This book is written on the assumption that they can and do, and most of what follows is concerned with establishing methods that will be helpful. In a nutshell, the teacher's role is to help children to see themselves as writers. Learning to write depends on seeing the point of that activity, on extending the range of real purposes for which it is used, on having available appropriate models and demonstrations of writing, and on a supporting environment that provides encouragement and appropriate audiences. How teachers fulfil this role is inevitably conditioned by their own expectations, and these are considered in the next chapter.

References

1   Janet Emig, 'Writing as a mode of learning', *College Composition and Communication*, May 1977, 28, p. 122.

2   Malcolm Ross, *Arts and the Adolescent*, London, Evans/ Methuen Educational, 1975, p. 47.

3   Sara W. Lundsteen *et al.*, *Help for the Teacher of Written Composition*, *New Directions in Research*, Urbana, Illinois, NCRE and ERIC, 1976, p. 9.

4   C. I. Rapstoff, 'The attitudes of teachers and their pupils to written expression', *Educational Review*, November 1964, 17, pp. 31–40.

5   Assessment of Performance Unit, *Language Performance in Schools*, Secondary Survey Report No. 1, London, HMSO, 1982, pp. 105–6.

6   Andrew Wilkinson *et al.*, *Assessing Language Development*, Oxford, Oxford University Press, 1980, p. 131.

7   J. J. Paquette, 'A study of the influence of sense of audience on the writing processes of eight adolescent boys', PhD thesis, London University Institute of Education, 1981.

8   Donald H. Graves, 'Children's writing: research directions and hypotheses based upon an examination of the writing processes of seven-year-old children', PhD dissertation, State University of New York, Buffalo, 1973.

9   Donald H. Graves, *Balance the Basics: let them write*, New York, Ford Foundation, 1978, pp. 14–15.

10 Her Majesty's Inspectorate, *Aspects of Secondary Education in England*, London, HMSO, 1979, p. 83.

11 Assessment of Performance Unit, *Language Performance in Schools*, Secondary Survey Report No. 1, London, HMSO, 1982, p. 107.

12 George Sampson, *English for the English*, Cambridge, Cambridge University Press, 1921; 1952 ed, p. 59.

13 *Guardian*, 28 November 1978; *The Times Educational Supplement*, 7 and 21 December 1979; *Guardian*, 13 March 1973.

2

THE TEACHER'S
EXPECTATIONS

The writing programmes we set up in school, the work that
we see as appropriate for children of different ages, abilities
and backgrounds, the way we evaluate the writing they do for
us will all be dominated by motives of which we are only
partly conscious. Our hidden criteria are instinctively un-
covered by the children; what we value is almost impercept-
ibly transmitted in our teaching. They learn with amazing
rapidity to provide us with what they think we want. Some
years ago in Nottingham, sickened by what seemed excessive
dependence of new first-formers on sentimental clichés (daf-
fodils waved their golden heads, lambkins frisked and the sun
sank in golden glory on every page), I decided to emphasize
precise observation. Armed with notebooks, the children were
taken to examine and describe the area at the back of the
school kitchens. (Lift the lid from the swill bins. How would
you describe the smell? What *sort* of noise do the flies make?
What vivid word ... ? and so on.) Unfortunately this activity
was construed as a teacher's overwhelming desire for social
realism, and writing on almost any topic thereafter began, 'As

I trudged through the mud of the gloomy alley, I could hear the rats scavenging in the dustbins, and the splintering of glass...'. To compare the published writing of city children of the 1930s with Chris Searle's *Stepney Words* in the 1970s is to see how differently pupils respond to changing models and teacher expectations.[1] In any place and at any time most children (though not all) will filter what they think and feel through their perceptions of what it is safe or tactful to provide for their teacher. The author Robert Westall has described this as 'pasteurised' writing:

> So we teach them to give us the pasteurised version; what they think is suitable for us to know. Polite small-talk. Right-wing teachers want polite small-talk about how to apply for a job by letter, or 'My favourite pet'. Left-wing teachers want polite small-talk about the sufferings of Angola or guerilla-children or East End tramps, none of whom the children are ever likely to meet, and about whom the only source of information is the left-wing teacher.

> Worse, long after the children have escaped our clutches physically, we retain our grasp on them psychologically.[2]

To develop as a teacher depends in part on progressively bringing to the surface the hidden expectations which we have. Otherwise we are stuck with inherited notions which grow steadily out of date or with instinctive feelings that cannot be justified. We can only discuss aims and methods rationally when we are more conscious of what is shaping our own mental models of the writing process. Consider some of the influences to which we are all subject and which continue to have a dominant effect on the ways in which we teach writing. Four of the most important ones can be briefly discussed.

Linguistic notions

When graduate students come to consider the teaching of the

mother tongue, they express the firmest convictions, though they frequently contradict one another. To take some actual examples, they write:

> The formal teaching of English grammar is unavoidable; it is essential to grasp the basics of any language in order to write lucidly and to express oneself accurately.

> Pupils should not be penalised for expressing themselves so-called incorrectly. It is a shame to link culpability with self-expression.

> Without a comprehensive grounding in vocabulary, grammar and sentence-construction no child will be able to communicate lucidly.

> The child should be given a free hand to express himself, providing he sticks to the rules laid down by convention and tradition.

Where have these absolute ideas (unavoidable, essential, no child...) come from? Like all of us, the students have been influenced by their own schooling (or their reactions against it), their reading, their university courses, articles in magazines, programmes on radio and television, comments of teacher friends, visits to classrooms and occasionally the findings of research. Their attitudes have more to do with faith, though, than with evidence. They tend to be related to dominant personality traits and to correlate with their social or political convictions. Some of our linguistic assumptions are so deeply emotionally embedded that they continue to dominate our teaching despite our rational awareness that they are not really valid. William Harpin gives such examples as a postgraduate English student who agreed that the findings of research on the negative effects of traditional grammar teaching on children's writing were conclusive, but still refused to accept them because he felt that such teaching had benefited *him* (and therefore should benefit all children).[3]

Frequently it is the superficial features of language that

arouse most concern, presumably because they are the most immediately identifiable. 'No split infinitive ever goes uncorrected', a teacher once proudly told me. Slang, missing apostrophes, sentences beginning with conjunctions or ending with prepositions – these are the flaws which we may have been taught to avoid and consequently which we see as most needing our attention. As W. H. Mittins has shown, though, there is simply no consensus over such issues as the correct use of 'due to', whether collective nouns are singular or plural, or whether it is permissible to say 'different to'.[4] Linguistic convictions at this level are based on the indefensible assumption that usage is governed by unchanging rules which have to be obeyed in all circumstances.

Half a century ago, the received wisdom for London teachers was that English had to be taught as 'a fine art'; a clear distinction had to be made between the undesirable 'language of the home and the street' and the approved 'language the school is trying to secure'. A pupil's writing should be based upon what he reads and hears 'in school' not on 'out of school life'.[5] Nowadays a teacher is more likely to be told that 'The starting point of English teaching is not language itself: the starting point is the experience of the kids' or that a child 'who is made ashamed of his own language habits suffers a basic injury as a human being'.[6] Such shifts in linguistic attitude imply radical changes in the kind of writing that is encouraged in schools.

Ideas of 'good' children's writing

It may seem obvious to say that we simultaneously define and refine our notions about the quality of writing and about desirable teaching procedures by looking critically at a wide range of what children have actually written in different circumstances, but such an idea is a relatively recent one. Working on assessment teams for the 16+, considering a school's CSE folders, examining case studies at in-service courses are all new developments. The flood of available published work by children is recent too, and before the 1920s it was almost unknown. Books on writing published early in this century illustrated their exercises with models, but these were always taken from established authors, often most inappropriate ones. 'Good' writing was to be like that of adults; the criterion for success was to avoid writing like children.

It is perhaps significant that in a lively and forward-looking book on the teaching of English, written in 1921, Philip Ballard chose to quote only one piece of children's writing (and that one actually dated from more than twenty years earlier). The work of a 14-year-old girl, who later became a headmistress, it is called 'a remarkable achievement' by Ballard, who says that he cites it as 'a sample of what is possible in an atmosphere of encouragement'. Part of this sample can give the flavour of the whole.

> The present is a time calculated to arouse the warmest feelings of loyalty and patriotism in the coldest heart that ever beat in a land governed by our beloved Queen...
>
> Never has the throne of Britain been filled by one so loving, so lovely, so truly queenly, and withal so womanly; so truly queen of home as well as State...
>
> Alone she stands on her glorious throne, supported as it is by her subjects' love, and wields her sceptre with a sway of gentleness and peace – a sway that, gentle as it is, has done more for England's weal than ever did tyrant's rod of iron.[7]

Ballard makes no attempt to explain what he sees as the merits of this piece; he simply assumes that readers will share his view.

If we ask why he found this essay outstanding, it seems clear that he must have admired the essentially adult 'voice', which sounds more like a leader-writer of *The Times* than a 14-year-old. It could be praised in terms of its fluent rhetoric, the extensive vocabulary, the variety of sentence construction to achieve specific purposes, the careful structure. One also suspects that the attitudes revealed in the writing were congenial to the girl's teachers and to Ballard. Significantly, he says that Miss Brace 'was encouraged by her teachers to express herself with the utmost freedom'. If this is true, then it shows how dominant the implied expectations of those teachers were. Reading the praise of this essay, and lacking alternative models, many other teachers must have assumed that this was the style and standard towards which they should urge their pupils. The fact that we now find it hard to take Miss Brace's essay seriously is not simply a comment on the way in which Ballard's views have dated in sixty years, it also throws light on *our* attitudes, our views of 'appropriate' children's styles, and our criteria for evaluation, of which more will be said later.

Books and materials in use

The teaching of writing in some schools appears to be dictated largely by what happens to be in the English stockroom at the time. To give out copies of *English Through Experience* or *The Art of English* means abandoning much of your curricular thinking to the author, and also inevitably taking on board some of that author's assumptions. The attitudes and expectations embodied in a course-book can dominate the working style of a class and the performance of pupils in it. They narrow a teacher's range of options: certain models of writing, methods of work, teacher roles and modes of evaluation become inevitable, and others are excluded. The same thing is true, of course, in a negative way. The calculated decision not to use *any* course book itself implies the rejection of certain attitudes towards writing, pupils and classroom practice (and, by implication, the adoption of others).

The assumptions that seem to underlie virtually all course-books are:

  i) That learning to write can be organized as an unvarying
        sequence of exercises and activities that is not affected by
        the student's success or failure at any point.

 ii) That all members of a class, of very different abilities and
        interests, will undertake the same activities at the same
        time.

iii) That students will not initiate ideas or activities, but that
        they and the teacher will accept the subordinate roles
        allocated to them.

For example, in one of the most popular courses, which has
sold over a million copies, comes this section:

> A class of the same age as you watched something burn.
> Here are some extracts from their Personal Writing ... [3
> passages] ... Personal Writing is writing for fun, for the
> pleasure that is in it. Now sit alertly and watch. Note
> particularly the colours, and exactly what happens, and use
> your sense of smell. Then, when you are told, write *freely
> and personally* about whatever comes into your mind.
> Don't describe what you saw and heard; write about your
> personal reactions to it.[8]

The assertions of freedom and personal response hardly
extend to the teacher, who is reduced to a kind of servo-
mechanism to the book, obediently lighting fires or producing
bottles at the appropriate moment. If it comes to that, the
pupils' freedom is also somewhat restricted. Told at one
moment to write 'freely and personally', they are then curtly
ordered *not* to describe what they saw and heard.

Even what are sometimes known as source books (*Reflec-
tions*, or *Contemporary English*) or collections of books,
cards, cassettes and slides, like the *Cambridge English Project*,
are not neutral packages of material. Without exercises or
direct teaching, the selection and organization, the proposed
activities, grow from a particular stance towards language
and towards teaching and learning. They only fit effectively

into a certain kind of classroom. It is in this way that books and materials influence our beliefs and practice. We may think that we are simply borrowing ideas or raw materials, but the acts of assessing what 'works' for us and how it works gradually modify our personal rationale.

Concepts of writing

Most subtly of all, perhaps, our practice is affected by the views of writing which we hold, by the terminology and concepts available to us for thinking and talking about the process. Students and less experienced teachers are frequently uneasy when asked to comment on children's written work, partly because they lack experience of such texts and partly because they doubt whether they have the appropriate terminology or forms of reference for describing them. They can, of course, apply the analytical categories developed in the study of English literature, seeing children's work through critical spectacles which suggest what writing 'ought' to be like. This was the way in which Ballard viewed the girl's essay quoted on page 22. No other concepts beyond those of genre and mode, of style and fluency and of accuracy of conventions were available to him. Because these have seemed so inadequate for describing what is happening in most children's writing, and for becoming more perceptive in responding to it, other frameworks of ideas with their own terminology have been developed in recent years. What is common to all of these is that they are grounded in the way that children *do* write (rather than how they *ought* to do so) and that they are concerned to discern the principles that underlie development of abilities in writing. In shifting the focus of attention from the reader's relationship with the text to the writer's, they have radically changed the way in which many teachers think.

It would be impossible to do justice to the authors (whose works are listed at the end of this volume) in a brief introduction of this kind, but three short examples can be given of the way in which our responses and our teaching methods can be influenced by the concepts available to us.

First, our awareness that first-formers frequently shift from past tense to present in mid-story, or from third person to first, or that they find predicting different outcomes in their own writing very difficult, has been made coherent by James Moffett's hypothesis that the language development of children is essentially concerned with their increasing ability to cope with abstraction, to handle greater distances in time and space between the writer, the reader and the experience. He sees the child developing the ability, reflected in the tenses of verbs, to move from the present and particular towards the abstract and the hypothetical. The most immediate and unpremeditated form is direct reporting of what *is happening*, followed by the more deliberately selected and organized reporting of what *happened*. In generalizing about what *happens*, the emphasis shifts from events to comparisons and categories. For Moffett, the most advanced stage is theorizing about what *will, may or could* happen: predicting, drawing conclusions and considering implications.[9] The practical implication of such a model is that shifting from straightforward narrative towards generalization, say, *necessarily* entails shifts in language use, and that therefore language 'skills' should be developed by choosing appropriate written activities and not by artificial exercises.

Second, the half-formed inklings of many teachers that children respond differently according to the person for whom they are writing have been given shape and point by the categories developed by Professor James Britton and others.

Following the suggestions in Moffett that one significant mark of increasing maturity in writing is the growth of a sense of audience, 'the ability to make adjustments and choices in writing which take account of the audience for whom the writing is intended', the team devised a similar classification on a continuum from private to public: writing for oneself, for the teacher, for a wider known audience and for an unknown, public audience.[10] Because the teacher is the self-nominated audience for so much of the work done in school, the division of the teacher-as-audience into four separate categories has clarified ideas considerably. The teacher may be perceived by writers in school as a trusted adult (to whom they can reveal their own thoughts and feelings), as a partner in a developing learning dialogue, who will make a personal response, as a professional mentor or as an examiner (concerned chiefly to assess). Such distinctions have already been influential in helping teachers to understand the effect of their implied relationships on the way in which their pupils write, and in calling attention to the way in which the *examiner* role becomes dominant in the upper forms of secondary schools (and throughout in certain subjects).

Again, at the practical level, awareness of the fact that pupils write differently for different audiences means that by varying the real or imaginary audiences for writing a teacher can extend the ways in which children write. We have also come to understand that many children's difficulties spring from our failure to define the audience for which their work is intended. Confusions in the books of eleven-year-olds frequently arise because they are unclear whether the notes they are making are meant to be a record for themselves, or an intelligible report for another pupil, or a proof to the teacher that the work has been understood.

Third, a number of educationalists have shifted attention from the writing, viewed as a virtually anonymous product, towards the writer as revealed in the work. A story, that is, can be seen not just in terms of its success in handling anti-climax or symbolic setting but for what it reveals about the author's emotional development, moral attitudes or sense of reality, or about the author's apprehension of the nature of the task, reactions to the teacher or response to the school ethos.

David Holbrook was one of the first to exemplify how a

serious reading of children's work involved almost inescap-
ably framing hypotheses or making judgements about the
writers' fears and wishes, their fantasies, emotional states and
values. In *English for the Rejected*,[11] his analysis of the
writing of lower stream students was accompanied by brief
comments from a psychiatrist, as though to symbolize a
different stance towards the understanding and assessment of
what has been written.

Holbrook's response to the potential of children who might
earlier have been dismissed, and Peter Abbs's concern for
English as an 'imaginative and aesthetic discipline'[12] have
been influential in directing attention to concepts of creativity.
Robert Witkin has made a systematic attempt to establish
categories for describing and discussing the origins of creative
expression.[13] He sees the child as progressively meeting new
levels of what he calls 'sensate experience' and symbolizing
these in one kind of 'holding form' or another on the way to a
final resolution. The four operations into which he analyses
the ordering of experience (establishing contrasts, sem-
blances, harmonies and discords) are applicable across the
arts, but this sense of a creative process in observable phases
can clearly affect the way in which as teachers we view the
writing of children.

These are examples only. Britton's function categories have
not been mentioned, nor Wilkinson's developmental model,
nor any of the linguistic categories for analysing discourse.
The purpose is simply to show that what we see in children's
writing depends on the questions we ask of it, the categories
we apply to it, or the framework that makes sense of it. We
teach according to the models we have in mind.

References

1   E.g. *Children's Verse*, an anthology of poems written by
    pupils of the elementary schools of Tottenham, Borough
    of Tottenham, 1937 and *Stepney Words* (1971),

London, Centreprise, 1973.

2 Robert Westall, 'The author in the classroom', *The Use of English*, Autumn 1979, 31, No. 1, p. 11.

3 William Harpin. 'Attitudes to language and language teaching', *English in Education*, Summer 1979, 13, No. 2, pp. 36–42.

4 W. H. Mittins, *Attitudes to English Usage*, Oxford, Oxford University Press, 1970.

5 *General Report on the Teaching of English in London Elementary Schools*, London, HMSO, 1929.

6 Harold Rosen, 'Up there where the linguists are', *The English Magazine*, 1979, No. 2, p. 7; M. A. K. Halliday et al., *The Linguistic Sciences and Language Teaching*, London, Longman, 1964.

7 P. B. Ballard, *Teaching the Mother Tongue*, London, Hodder and Stoughton, 1926, pp. 69–70.

8 A. W. Rowe and Peter Emmens, *English Through Experience*, Book 1, St Albans, Blond, 1963.

9 James Moffett, *Teaching the Universe of Discourse*, Boston, Mass., 1968.

10 James Britton et al., *The Development of Writing Abilities 11–18*, London, Macmillan, 1975.

11 David Holbrook, *English for the Rejected*, Cambridge, Cambridge University Press, 1964.

12 Peter Abbs, *Root and Blossom*, London, Heinemann, 1976.

13 Robert Witkin, *The Intelligence of Feeling*, London, Heinemann, 1974.

3

TENSIONS FOR THE
ENGLISH TEACHER

Between different views of writing

Only a few members of a school staff are likely to have strong
opinions about the teaching of physics or German; most of
them will have views about the teaching of writing. English
teachers come under pressure because their business is
everybody's business; they cannot operate in isolation. Because there is no general agreement about where and how
English fits into the curriculum, English teachers are likely to
be pulled in different directions by conflicting views of their
responsibilities.

When the DES presented a model of different 'areas of
experience' that should be involved in a common curriculum,
it was clear that – unlike other subjects – English might claim
to contribute to virtually all of those areas in differing
degrees: aesthetic and creative, ethical, linguistic, physical,
scientific, social and political, or spiritual.[1] In some schools
which are organized by Faculties, English comes under the
heading Humanities, in others Languages and Literature, and
Peter Abbs has recently argued that the real place of English is

with the Expressive Arts.[2] Each of these locations, though, would seem to put a different emphasis on the kinds of writing for which the English teacher would be chiefly responsible. The apparent openness of syllabus ('You can teach anything and call it English') brings inevitable problems of definition, particularly in the teaching of writing.

English teachers are likely to come under pressure in two main ways from colleagues outside their own Department. First, it may be suggested that the writing they encourage is not 'real' work, concerned with learning. Dealing with children's out of school experience, often apparently trivial in itself, can be perceived as a waste of time. Indeed, it is sometimes suggested that writing in English is dangerous and subversive because pupils are encouraged to express feelings that are hostile to school or that undermine discipline. It has even been said that the fact that children enjoy writing in English somehow makes it harder for teachers to get them to write in 'more demanding' ways in other subjects.

Second, some teachers may be eager to abdicate from any responsibility for the language of their pupils, and try to suggest that writing is wholly the preserve of the English staff. In staff-rooms, it is still possible to hear remarks like 'It's my job to teach history: you're here to teach them how to write' or 'I have to dictate notes because you haven't taught them how to make their own' or 'Why can't you teach them how to spell the words they need in my subject?' or 'How can they be expected to learn French grammar if you never teach English grammar?'. The implication of comments like these is that English should fulfil a service function, and that the teacher becomes – in Peter Abbs's phrase – 'a man carrying a bag of tools but with only other people's jobs to do'.[3]

Both kinds of pressure which have been mentioned arise from uncertainty about how far English teachers are responsible for the writing done by pupils in all areas of the curriculum. How far are we concerned with children learning to write, and how far with the connected but different process of writing to learn? To assert that English is a self-contained discipline can be seen as unhelpful to our colleagues. Their resentment can be intensified by the intolerance (even contempt) which some English teachers display for the writing practices of other subjects, and by the bland assurance that English has all the curricular answers. On the other hand, if the English teachers offer themselves as advisers on language to the whole staff, they can be accused of interference and of trying to impose unsuitable methods on others. Once relationships have become hostile, motives are always suspect.

Such tensions spring directly from the organizational pattern of secondary education, with its separation of departments and of the teachers within them. Very early after transfer from primary school, children come to see marked differences between the writing they do in English and that which is required in other school subjects. One second-year boy summed it up: 'In English I write what I feel, in History I write about the past.' 12- and 13-year-olds saw an antithesis between 'writing down your own thoughts', 'expressing your feelings and points of view', or working 'from your imagination' in English and the emphasis on objective, dispassionate fact elsewhere in the curriculum. 'In science you say only exactly what you saw'; 'in other subjects you write about the facts and nothing else'. A girl and a boy from the third year expressed it like this:

> In most English work you can put your own views, thoughts, etc, into the piece, but in other subjects, especially sciences, it is wrong and often pointless to do this.

> In English you are encouraged to write what you feel but in other subjects you have to write what you know. In other subjects you use an objective style and try not to let emotion cloud your work but in English you use a subjective style.

Teachers' expectations of writing are perceived as different, because the purposes of the writing are not the same. 'In science subjects we don't bother so much how we write it – the teachers aren't fussy', remarked a second-year girl, and 'My history teacher is more interested in my history facts than my grammar', said a third year. By contrast, 'In English I take more care with what I write and make the writing more imaginative.'

> In English you try to use different styles, you use more adult-type words or rearrange the words in a different way. Whereas in other subjects the style has got to be more simple ... there is no place for flights of fancy.

Much writing outside English was described as borrowing the language of teacher or text-book. Third-year pupils said:

> In English there are no strict guidelines, but in other subjects ... you are just writing up notes, you are given the straight facts and are expected to insert words here and there to make sentences.

> In other subjects you take words from books or the blackboard...

> In English you can express yourself but in other subjects we just copy off the board and all answer the same questions.

In one school where I examined all the writing done by a group of pupils aged 11 to 13 over two terms, it appeared that only in English did they ever write connectedly in their own words. All the remainder – a great deal of actual writing – was copied notes, formal exercises or blank filling.

Are we conditioning pupils into this apparent belief that there is an inevitable gulf between writing done in English and elsewhere? Do they see English as concerned exclusively with personal, imaginative work, to the exclusion of other language functions? How far should English teachers adapt their programmes according to the views of writing held and practised by other members of staff? How do they reconcile the tensions between their departmental and their school responsibilities? Currently three different answers seem to be offered in schools:

(*i*) CO-OPERATION BETWEEN DEPARTMENTS

The fashionable answer would be to insist that the English teacher is one of a team and that to act in isolation is to weaken the school's work. Unfortunately, despite all the lip-service paid to Language Across the Curriculum, very few schools have been able to progress towards a coherent agreed language policy. Even to agree on a code of marking symbols has been too much for some of them. A co-operative strategy has to originate in staff agreement; a young teacher can hardly initiate it.

(*ii*) ACCEPTANCE OF THE UNIQUENESS OF ENGLISH

Some teachers will argue that instead of worrying about the different language demands of different subjects, English teachers should simply concentrate on what they do best and what interests them most, on the grounds that every activity in an English lesson is somehow extending pupils' command of language. Indeed, they should capitalize on the fact that writing in English *is* seen as different by their pupils, and preferred by most of them to what they have to do in other subjects. Peter Medway has argued cogently that other subjects should accept what marks off the best English practice, which 'under the guise of just another curriculum subject' has actually applied a different model of education:

knowledge to be made, not given; knowledge comprising more than can be discursively stated; learning as a diverse range of processes, including affective ones; educational processes to be embarked on with outcomes unpredictable; students' perceptions, experiences, imaginings and unsystematically acquired knowledge admitted as legitimate curricular content.[4]

(*iii*) DIAGNOSIS AND PLANNING

A middle course, sometimes contemptuously referred to as filling in the blanks, may be a more effective compromise. Precisely because of the lack of specified content, English is free to supply what is missing elsewhere. A teacher can discover what language uses are *not* being developed elsewhere and work particularly at these. For example, if most transactional subject writing is at the lower levels of recording and reporting, perhaps English teachers should be giving more attention to activities which encourage pupils to speculate, persuade and theorize. At least such a stance assumes that English teachers might change their practice if other teachers were to accept responsibility for the language used in learning their subjects.

Even within the English Department, though, teachers are likely to vary in their views of the writing process, and to choose different courses of action according to the models of writing which they hold.

The old arguments may still go on about whether the dominant concern of the English teacher should be to develop, on the one hand, creativity and 'powers of imagination', or, on the other, writing skills, accuracy and precision. Put like that, with a suggestion of either/or, it is clearly a false polarization: originality and precision are both necessary. 'Back to basics!' is a cry which suggests that somewhere along the line we have abandoned them.

The English teacher who is wedded to the notion of creativity as the supreme principle will probably reject any planned programme as 'cramping'; work must be wholly flexible so that it can be adapted to the shifting needs, experiences and reactions of individual pupils. In these terms, all learning situations are unique; each individual has to exploit a series of one-off experiences as seems best in the light of the moment. 'Creative writing' is defined not in terms of the writing done but of the techniques used to obtain it. Because originality cannot be taught, by definition, the teacher's role is pushed back to providing the initial stimulus and enthusiasm.[5]

A different teacher may have a writing programme organized in detail and structured to develop particular language functions (those imposed by the demands of the 'real' world, to which students must conform). Writing is defined in terms of those demands and of the language appropriate to meet them; the teacher's role is to define, guide, correct. Neither of these teachers is necessarily better or worse than the other. Both of them may have an over-restrictive view of the place of writing in school.

The problem for students or young teachers is that they are likely to be bombarded with conflicting statements of strong opinion. The nearest we can come to offering advice is to propose a period of quiet agnosticism. Look at the children's work rather than listening to the comments about it. Do not be pushed into a neat pigeon-hole of someone else's making. Try not to be trapped into either/or arguments. Avoid assuming that what you have not attempted cannot work. Do not imagine that this year's convictions will be unchanged next year.

Between freedom and control

It is clear from what pupils say and write that one of the great attractions about English is the openness both of the work and of their relationships with teachers.

> It is the subject which I think gives you most freedom. (girl, 15)

> No-one else can tell you what to write and how to feel. (girl, 15)

The teacher leaves ourselves to ourselves ... she lets us do what we think about ... it's our choice. (boy, 14)

In English you can find something that's your own. (boy, 12)

You can use your own imagination ... you can put what you like really, it's your story. (boy, 12)

This freedom, commented on in a number of surveys as contributing to pupils' relatively favourable view of English as a subject,[6] is equally cherished by most English teachers. It can, however, come under threat when misunderstood. Parents have complained when adolescents were asked to imagine a day in the life of an IRA bomber, or the feelings of a girl contemplating an abortion. One teacher has been suspended for publishing a collection of children's writing without permission from the school governors.

Freedom of expression can lead to problems, especially for students and less experienced teachers. Three problems, in particular, need thinking about. First, how does the teacher deal with highly personal or confessional writing? Second, what is to be done about work that the teacher finds objectionable, rude or obscene? Third, how far can children be permitted the freedom of individual choice in a classroom situation? Each of these three, in very different ways, raises problems about the teacher's role in relationship with pupils. English makes it impossible to separate out teaching and pastoral concern or guidance.

INTIMATE WRITING

First there are the more personally revealing pieces of writing done for the teacher-as-trusted-adult (to use Britton's term). Take as an example this poem by a 16-year-old boy in a Midlands comprehensive school.

Close but not touching

I am an eighth of an inch from her
   eyebrow and I see on her
skin the imprint of each day and
her breath is warm and damp and
I feel vibrations in her throat and
   I can't get any closer.

I want to flow in her blood
   climb her bones
then see from behind her eyes
   walk with her legs
   feel with her hands
   take her apart and
   know her all and
   combine with her but
I can't get any closer.

God bury me beneath Time
   with her because my life
   isn't enough time to find
   a way to her
      through her mind
   to want her with anything but lust
   that can't get any closer but must
   before youth's beauty hardens
      mind as well as face
   and age's granite door
      slams shut in my face.

Read impersonally, as here on the printed page, it can be
unemotionally considered as a young man's attempt to make
his half-felt, half-understood apprehensions more articulate
and explicit. Read by a teacher who knows both the
individuals involved, though, the situation is different. It's not
just the privacy of the feelings (not a poem for reading aloud
to the class) but the question of *why* you've been given it. Is it

to bring something into the open, to explain his recent behaviour, to provoke a reaction, to strike a romantic pose, or is it simply a literary exercise? The teacher's hypothesis, based on previous knowledge of the person, will dictate reactions to the writer as well as to the writing, and thus affect the developing relationship between teacher and pupil. And even at the strictly pedagogic level, what do you say to an individual who brings you work as personal as this? How do you help him to estimate what he has achieved? What would you particularly praise? Would you criticize any aspects of the poem and, if so, which? How would you try to aid further development? What reading might you propose? Our response to personal work reveals us unerringly. Children instinctively recognize the teacher who is always talking about 'personal relationships' but cannot get on with anyone else in the staff-room, who invites 'frankness' but whose experience of life is too limited and immature to be relied on.

Distinct from such revelatory writing is the personal work that is designed deliberately or subconsciously to manipulate the relationship between pupil and teacher, and which raises issues of professional behaviour. How far does the 'trusted-adult' role confer the confidentiality of the confessional? Sexual proposals, of a greater or lesser degree of explicitness, can usually be defused rapidly by humour or bluntness. Increasing suggestions of intimacy, drawing the teacher into unsolicited confidences, are harder to deal with, because less obvious. A teacher can be nudged into a situation of shared secrets and allusions which can suggest that one pupil has a special and favoured relationship. The teacher's support may be enlisted for good or bad reasons. It is often hard to distinguish between self-dramatization and a cry for help. When a boy complains of being bullied, is it an expression of genuine need, or an excuse for bad work, or an attempt to get revenge on a classmate? When a girl talks of brutal ill-treatment by her mother, is it a case for the NSPCC or fantasy built out of last night's quarrel? It is rarely possible to answer these questions from the writing itself; you have to know the individuals involved.

The same is even more true of the work we might categorize as obsessional. One girl I taught contrived to bring into every piece, often with no regard for plausibility, a mother–daughter relationship in which the mother was always assaulted, wounded or mutilated and eventually died. Holbrook gives other examples and, indeed, has written a chapter with the title, 'Is English teaching "therapy"?'[7] – though he understandably does not give a direct answer to his question. In cases like these, the teacher's responsibility must be to call in expert advice. We are not trained as alienists. Unfortunately we are also often ill-prepared for dealing with the much more elementary emotional needs of children because our own feelings are immature and inhibited. Awareness of this *may* help us to be more understanding.

PROVOCATIVE WRITING

So far we have considered work that could raise problems by its intimacy, because the teacher has to consider how much 'distance' it is essential to keep from the pupil. Now it is necessary to think about work that often relishes or emphasizes the separation between child and teacher, that can be seen as testing out, or as a threat. Surprisingly little is ever said about this in books or conferences, though many (perhaps most) students have to grapple with the problem, because it is particularly challenging to those who are least confident in their role.

What happens when 'free expression' comes to mean the expression of ideas or attitudes that we dislike or despise?

Todays problem is that all the imergants come over and goes into social security get paid every week and if they have got no home they put them in 5 star hotels.

Black people should not be allowed in England because

England is meant for whites. England is nearly full of black people. They should be thrown out of England ... Blacks do some of the queerest things you ever known. They are even putting black people on telly and whites invented it so only whites should go on the telly.[8]

Liberal-minded students launch into projects dealing with nuclear disarmament or crime and punishment and exclaim with dismay that – in the words of one – 'I've got a class of fascists!' because when they are asked to write their own opinions the children advocate flogging, hanging and using the H-bomb. Sometimes – though not always – the reason is all too clear: the teacher's convictions are so strong that any independently minded child will be driven into opposition.

The Leavis-O'Malley–Thompson tradition saw an educational duty in fighting against certain features in society that were de-humanizing (advertising, the popular press, triviality in books and entertainment) and talked of the need to teach *against* the values of some homes. For teachers in this tradition the school itself was a substitute home. Nowadays the dragons to be fought may be more frequently seen in socio-political terms, but the implication that in English we are somehow teaching *values* is still widespread. If that is interpreted as inculcating our own convictions, rather than genuinely opening issues for discussion, then we are likely to provoke resistance.

Unguarded remarks like, 'Yes, of course you must write just what you think' usually reveal that the teacher is not aware of the subtext beneath the words that children are saying. 'Do we write the actual words of the characters?' means 'Can we use swear-words?' Similarly 'Do you want a full description?' can leave unsaid 'because if so I'm going to produce a piece of soft porn'. The press regularly reports disastrous occasions when such writing is dragged into the open, as when two 16-year-old boys were suspended from school for writing what one of them called 'a load of stupid, obscene words with an obscene story around them ... about sex with all the usual four-letter words. ... We wrote it for fun'.[9] Experienced teachers, who know the game and choose their words carefully, get little sex-and-violence writing except from disturbed individuals. Women students, though, do receive stories in which central characters (not infrequently women teachers) are attacked by gangs, raped, disembowelled or torn apart by motor bikes. Such writing (unless it becomes obsessive) has to be seen as part of the testing-out process which a new teacher undergoes and not over-dramatized.

When children write about school, as they are often urged to do, it is frequently difficult to draw the line between acceptable or justified comment and deliberate provocation in what they present. Do we forbid *any* personal comments on other members of staff? Do we allow favourable remarks but ban criticism? Do we try to draw a line between commentary and impertinence? There is the additional danger that written comments may be seen by other teachers whose attitudes may differ from your own. Should we accept or question such comments as the following, for example?

> The headmaster moans at us, and he stands up there, and he thinks he's God
>
> I think the RE teacher's a queer
>
> I hate Mr _____ ... he hit my friend for no reason
>
> Mr _____ goes into the girls' toilets
>
> Sometimes I could kill _____ one day I'm going to say stuff you to him.

On what principles do we make our decisions? How can we best tackle such comments when they appear? Do we ask, 'Would you mind if I told Mr _____ that you'd written this?' More to the point, how do we prevent the problem from arising, in the instructions we give?

Teachers have different strategies for dealing with work

that expresses attitudes which they find distasteful, and no one of these is the universal answer. They might advise a young teacher, for example, in different cases:

 i) Simply ignore the attitudes, thus depriving the writer of the expected confrontation. Mark all the errors of spelling and punctuation in detail.

 ii) Present the issue for discussion or debate in class, thus bringing the matter into the open, where different reactions can be expressed.

iii) Set as the next piece of work the rewriting of the theme or story from the viewpoint of the victim or minority group under attack.

iv) Provide information for group study that refutes the opinions expressed.

 v) See the problem as one of relationships. Get to know the individual better, and then talk honestly about what you see as the difficulty.

FREEDOM OF CHOICE

Organizationally, the tension between freedom and control is manifested in uncertainty about the amount of choice pupils should be offered (about what to write, when to write and perhaps whether to write), the stages at which their choices are seen as valid, and the balance between what may be thought of as 'public' and 'private' writing. The school environment is inevitably an artificial context for much writing (see pages 59–65). Under what circumstances should children have the right to say that their work is not to be read by other pupils, or even by the teacher? What are the balancing advantages and disadvantages of a system in which children are encouraged to keep a personal notebook which is unsupervised and only shared at the wish of the author? Most English teachers, consciously or unconsciously, work on a pattern which divides the work of a group into 'my time' (teacher directed, deliberately structured) and 'their time' (providing freedom to choose topics, approaches, styles), and which assumes that the proportion of 'their time' increases as the children get older, are more capable of making deliberate choices, and have acquired the ability to set themselves appropriate projects. In practice, the amount of teacher-directed work seems to decrease in the first three years of secondary school, and then often to increase again as public examinations draw nearer.

One source of tension which results from increased freedom of choice is that the teacher has to organize a classroom in which different pupils will have clashing needs. Individuals or groups are likely to be simultaneously at different stages of different projects, some of them wanting to be quiet to think or to get on with writing that is already advanced, others anxious to try out passages on friends, some seeking ideas and guidance. It will be impossible to prevent noise and movement in such a classroom. How does the teacher prevent the situation from becoming – in a teacher's phrase – 'like a wet break'? This is considered in more detail on pages 60–5. As with most real teaching problems, there is no simple answer. If the room is arranged with the pupils in small groups and tables, there may not be too many difficulties. In a large class-room, there may be a 'quiet end' to which pupils can withdraw to work on their own, and if rooms and teacher-time can be planned more flexibly, the problem virtually disappears. Observation suggests, though, that success largely depends on a teacher who can be relaxed in such an open situation with a group of pupils who have learned over a period of time the advantages of a co-operative manner of working.

References

1 Department of Education and Science, Green Paper, *Education in Schools: A Curriculum Document*, London, HMSO, 1977.

2 Peter Abbs, 'The reconstitution of English as art', in Malcolm Ross, *The Aesthetic Imperative*, Oxford, Pergamon, 1981.

3 Ibid., p. 103.

4 Peter Medway, *Finding a Language*, London, Writers and Readers, 1980, p. 10.

5 For a fuller discussion, see Robert Protherough. 'When in doubt, write a poem', *English in Education*, Spring 1978, 12, No. 1, pp. 9–21.

6 E.g. Schools Council, *Young School Leavers*, London, HMSO, 1968; Robert Witkin, *The Intelligence of Feeling*, London, Heinemann, 1974; M. Stubbs and S. Delamont, *Explorations in Classroom Observation*, Chichester, John Wiley, 1976.

7 David Holbrook, *English in Australia Now*, Cambridge, Cambridge University Press, 1973.

8 Originally quoted in the Journal of the National Association for Multi-Racial Education and cited in the *Observer* (22 January 1978), the *Guardian* (6 February 1978) and *English in Education*, Spring 1977, 11, No. 1.

9 The *Guardian*, 12 May 1971.

Conclusion

The thrust of this Rationale has been to suggest that thinking about one's own views of writing and of learning to write is an essential preliminary to deciding how to teach writing. A number of difficult questions have been asked, but no definite answers can be given to some of them. On some issues, the principles and the evidence are clear; on others, teachers have to work out their own answers to fit their own circumstances. What matters crucially is *awareness*. Teachers who have consciously considered the influences which have shaped their own language attitudes, who have looked with understanding at children and their work, who have thought about different models of writing and who have critically examined materials and methods in use, have done what they can to prepare themselves professionally. Such awareness will not of itself make them good teachers, but it should at least make them less likely to be bad ones. What follows in Part Two considers the more obviously practical issues of planning, initiating, aiding and responding to children's writing.

PART TWO:
PRACTICE

4

PLANNING THE PROGRAMME

Establishing goals

This part of the book grapples with the problem: 'How do you teach someone else to write?' Whatever answer we give, even if it is brutally 'You can't!' will depend on our views of what success means, both in terms of learning to write and in terms of the teacher's involvement in that process. We are concerned, that is, with defining goals, with what people want to happen, with establishing our order of priorities, and that involves asking four preliminary questions.

(1) Who sets the goals? Teachers sometimes assume that this is their responsibility alone. In the case of writing particularly, however, parents, employers, universities, politicians, the children themselves all have conscious or subconscious, positive or negative assumptions about what *should* be done. It is the conflict between these (and, indeed, between educators themselves) that causes difficulty for English teachers. They may well agree with Peter Abbs that English teaching is 'an imaginative and aesthetic discipline',[1] but the

Engineering Industry Training Board ignores the imaginative
and aesthetic when listing the eight basic skills of writing (to
be neat, to spell correctly, to prepare written messages, to
write simple formal letters, to prepare notes, to write technical reports ...).[2] Schools are judged by their success or
failure in achieving the often contradictory aims set by
different groups: can the children write a good business letter?
a formal essay? an original poem? an exciting story? can they
get good grades at O-level? at A-level? can they spell and
punctuate accurately? can they make clear notes and sum-
maries? can they use complex sentences fluently?

(2) How specific should the goals be? Goals are there for
achieving: directly or by implication they control the programme of work. Most teachers operate simultaneously with
long-term wide goals for a term or a year and short-term
narrow ones for a week or a period. Framing each of these has
its own opposed dangers: such a high degree of generality that
nothing is conveyed but good intentions ('to encourage
imaginative, creative expression') or narrowing objectives to
the level of exercises ('to enable students to combine two
simple sentences by using relative clauses'). To convert the
activities themselves into goals, as some lists of behavioural
objectives and some course books do, restricts the range of
work and ignores the differences between individual students
and teachers. Goals have to be expressed in terms which are
open enough for teachers to make their own professional
decisions about which materials and methods will be most
appropriate for their students as individuals.

(3) What sort of connection is there between goals and
teaching styles? The most obvious demonstration of the
connection is perhaps the washback effect of assessment, as
teachers work within the objectives of the examination
system: 'Don't choose an argumentative topic: it's harder to
get a good grade'; 'Write something else, you've got enough
stories in your folder already'. David Holbrook quoted a
teacher's remark to a 14-year-old pupil: 'You are not to think

like this before "O" level.'[3] Activities and attitudes designed to encourage children to express their personal feelings freely will not be the same as those intended to foster clear and precise reporting or those inviting children to 'become' another person and see through their eyes or those which are meant to develop analytic skills in writing. As Gordon Wells put it concisely, 'different curricular goals call for different styles of linguistic interaction'.[4]

(4) Who knows about the goals? Some English teachers behave as though aims are a shameful secret, to be kept strictly private, rather than an agreed focus for the work of the Department. At the simplest and widest, most would probably express the long-term goal of learning to write in such words as: the development of those abilities which enable a boy or girl to write fluently, accurately and effectively according to the appropriate audience for the whole range of purposes required in life. Where there is much less agreement is in translating such a global aim into short-term aims seen in terms of curriculum. The students as well as the staff need to be conscious of these. Precisely because writing demands such a complex range of abilities, it is particularly desirable that students should be made aware of specific, attainable goals, and should be conscious of progressing towards them. What principles then should underlie the programme which is to achieve the goals, however they are formulated?

Some principles underlying the teaching of writing

(1) Writing involves two activities. Children (or adults) who are writing are engaged in two quite different processes simultaneously. They are thinking of something, composing words in their heads, and then they are writing those words down. The two processes are not inseparable. The words could be dictated to another person or put on to tape and transcribed. The results might not be identical, but one

investigation found that in adults the differences between these methods of recording were insignificant: 'Composition, acquired with difficulty over years, appears to be the fundamental skill.'[5] It is important for teachers to keep this separation in mind. The ability to compose can be helped by talking to others (and indeed, talking to oneself) or by retelling (as in an oral culture) the words of others. Oral composition, like written, involves putting thoughts into words and sentences; grammar can be improved through speech (as parents of small children are well aware). The mechanical task of writing is transcribing from one's own dictation. It is in this second process that spelling and punctuation become important: they are features of written transcription, not of composition. 'A written composition is some edited version of a person's inner speech.'[6]

(2) Writers depend on reading. The ability to compose in words that are appropriate for writing, not speech, depends on awareness that has come first from listening to books read aloud and then from first-hand reading. The crucial sense of what it means to be a writer, of what writing *can* do, only comes through progressive exposure to print. Children's previous verbal experience determines what is available for them to commit to paper. In addition, the ability to revise – which written composition makes possible in a way that the spoken does not – depends on the writer (possibly helped by someone else) reading back critically what has been written.

(3) Children learn to write by writing. What has been said about the importance of reading does not diminish the truth of the old aphorism that children learn to write by writing: that is, by writing complete experiences, stories, poems, articles. There is absolutely no evidence that the writing process can be broken down into neat sequences of small units, that doing exercises can somehow 'prepare' children to write better, that instruction in 'skills' is essential before they can ever be creative. They write better by writing more for different purposes and for different audiences on as many

occasions as possible. This means, of course, that perceptible improvement is often slow, and extends over a considerable period of time. Nevertheless, the only real indicator of progress is to compare pieces of writing done over a period. Increased success in tests of sentence combining or error correction is no assurance of better performance in free writing.

(4) 'Real' writing involves the children's own choices and language. The HMI Survey found that fourth- and fifth-year pupils did a vast amount of writing – even average pupils managed something like 30,000 words each term – but that much of this was 'a re-presentation of teacher or text book language', from dictation, copying or exercises. Little was demanded that would help pupils 'to feel that their individual reactions were valued, or that their variations of information or opinion were welcome'.[7] A primary teacher made a crisp distinction between those schools where 'real' writing was encouraged and those where it was not.

> In schools where writing isn't real, where the teacher or the school makes the decisions at every stage of the writing procedure, children are expected merely to practise and perform. They are not involved in making choices for themselves, their purpose isn't their own, they are not real writers.[8]

Though the polarizing is perhaps too neat, and though many children do seem to find their own purposes and satisfactions within teacher-controlled situations, the emphasis of the article is right. Children need the opportunities to be like 'real' writers: to explore what they are really thinking and feeling, to make their own choices about the mode of expression and to share the results if they wish. Graves has shown that in these circumstances even young children write more than in formal settings.[9] To see school writing as different by definition from writing outside the school is to undermine the learning process.

(5) Children come to writing by different routes and at different speeds. Writing is an individual process; no two responses to any written assignment are the same; no two students have absolutely identical problems in learning to write. It is no longer possible – if it ever was – to conceive of a school writing programme in which all students of the same age carry out the same activities in the same order. We have to expect that different pupils will follow different routes, though the goals to be reached and the principles governing their journeys will be the same. Nevertheless much of our organization and practice denies the case against uniformity that was so strongly argued sixty years ago:

> It is, of course, quite absurd to demand that all boys in a class must be writing on the same subject at the same time. ... For his composition exercise a boy has a reasonable right to choose the subject – so has the teacher; and justice should be done to both. Each must give and take. ... The starting of a composition exercise, so to speak, by pistol-shot, with the understanding that all the runners must get to the tape in much the same time (without handicap) is a damnable inheritance from the tyranny of examinations.[10]

The useful work now being done on establishing 'staging posts' or developmental ladders in writing ability (see pages 78*ff*) is not intended to establish a curricular pattern for whole classes. It implies a form of management which monitors what individuals do, which prescribes specific guidance to aid progress, and which matches students with a choice of appropriate assignments from a wide selection.

(6) A fear of writing may have to be overcome. It is not writing itself but the circumstances which surround it, the formal separation from other activities, that are frightening. No wonder George Sampson said, 'let us abolish composition from the curriculum!'[11] Many English graduates, asked to write about their responses to a piece of music, confess to

feelings of panic: they do not know what the tutor's expectations are; it's an unfamiliar task; they are surrounded by other people instead of writing privately in their own rooms. Many of us are conscious of the alarm created by having to make the first marks on a blank sheet of paper, or knowing that there is a time limit within which we have to complete a letter or memorandum. For children, the insecurity is much more understandable. Many of them early in the secondary school have learned that they write poorly, that writing is drudgery, that avoiding mistakes is the most important thing and that what they are interested in or good at is largely ignored in English lessons. In the face of such negative reactions, good teachers labour first of all to create a climate in the classroom that lessens the fear, reduces the sense of being threatened, and encourages children to trust in and develop their own language resources. The personality of the teacher is clearly crucial. When pupils are asked what marks teachers who have helped them to write, they pick out such qualities as warmth and enthusiasm, interest in them as individuals (and not just in their work), encouragement of active participation, welcoming of questioning and tolerance of uncertainty. The first weeks with a new group are vital in establishing this atmosphere of confidence. Ideally children should be asked to write on subjects about which they have considerable knowledge or experience, in ways which enable them to feel comfortable about expressing themselves, and at levels where they can experience success. Confidence is an essential ingredient in developing skill.

Some models of school writing

In the 1960s most teachers operated within the assumptions of a model which suggested a simple polar opposition between two kinds of writing, the 'creative', mostly in English, and factual 'content' or 'subject' writing. The differences would have been summed up in terms like these:

Creative writing	Subject writing
1 Emphasis on creative activity, original self-revelation through language.	Emphasis on accurate conveying of information, of what has been learned.
2 Concerned with imaginative response to personal experiences and feelings.	Concerned with acceptance of 'objective' facts and ideas.
3 Structure grows organically, as one discovers what one wishes to say.	Structure is logically pre-planned and organized to communicate an agreed message.
4 The creative act seen as almost magical, spontaneous, inexplicable and virtually unteachable.	Writing seen as a task that can be broken down into a learning sequence.
5 Assessment based on originality, vividness, truth to experience.	Assessment based on achievement of agreed objectives, clarity, accuracy.

Such a model can be criticized as misleading rather than as wholly false. By emphasizing two extremes of writing it disguised the fact that actually there is a continuum of many writing modes and tasks stretching between them. It tended to push English teachers towards one particular kind of writing activity to the exclusion of others. By directing attention to differences in writing practices it switched attention away from the teacher's role in the process. Perhaps most seriously of all, by emphasizing the marked points of difference, the model concealed the similarities and disregarded what might mark off the teaching of both these modes from other possible methods.

In fact, from the teaching point of view, 'creative' and 'subject' writing lessons looked extremely similar. An observer would notice four stages:

1 The teacher provided the initial material: an experiment, a poem, information, a stimulus, maps, etc.
2 The teacher gave instructions for the written task.
3 The children wrote.
4 The teacher collected the writing and marked it.

The unspoken assumptions were that the teacher was dominant in initiating the work, and that the children were to take on board what they were given or to respond to the stimulus which the teacher had chosen. The writing was the children's part, and the teacher was then only involved in giving spellings or reminding them to write in paragraphs. Writing was done for the teacher and against the clock. Whether the work was a poem written in response to hearing a piece of music or an essay based on information about the causes of the French Revolution, the success of individuals and of the lesson was to be judged by the work given in at the end.

Increasingly, English teachers have come to question many of the assumptions underlying that model. Individuals have stressed such principles as:

i) Giving the children more autonomy in initiating topics and in developing ways of working, so that everyone is not necessarily engaged on the same activity.

ii) More interaction between children, in planning the work and in deciding how tasks should be set up, seeing writing as a more collaborative activity.

iii) More attention to the process of writing itself, and the establishing of fruitful ways in which the teacher can intervene in it.

iv) Concern for development of the work through redrafting and shaping ideas.

v) More attention to writing for real audiences other than the teacher.

vi) More sharing and discussion of work between children.

vii) Evaluation of the work concerned more with the process (what happens to the children) as well as the end-product.

There is no single, universally accepted model of what writing in English should be like. Indeed, the 1970s were characterized precisely by the rejection of the notion that any one model could be universally applicable. The situation is not wholly relative though. Some models *are* likely to be more effective than others. Australian enquiries have suggested that in their schools two opposing networks of ideas about the teaching of writing are current. Some teachers shared what might be termed a 'skills' model, concerned with isolating particular 'basics' for instruction, testing student learning of these skills, in a teacher dominated situation with absolute ideas of 'good' English. Others shared a 'growth' model, marked by the importance attached to relationships and motivation, sequential links between personal and writing development, an importance attached to talk, and the teacher as writer and sharer as well as instructor. Patrick Diamond's research, comparing the work of students over a year in classes taught by teachers committed to one or other of these models, concluded that the models did affect performance. Consistent implementation of the 'skills-based' model was associated with an appreciable decline in class results; whereas the 'growth' model 'has been shown ... to be comparatively productive in terms of a class's writing performance'.[12]

If we consider what the sequence of stages for whole-class work with a 'growth' model teacher would be, compared with the four-stage process previously mentioned, it would probably look more like this:

1 Opener and focus: direct experience, anecdote, poem, film, etc.
2 Classroom conversation, possibly in groups or pairs, collecting, relating, jotting, formulating.
3 Defining the task: pupils considering what they are going to write, how and for whom.
4 Writing a first draft and discussing it with partner, group or teacher, considering possible changes. Teacher may read some drafts aloud and encourage positive responses and suggestions.
5 Revised draft(s), changing, extending and proof-reading. Possibly a 'fair copy' produced.

6 Publication and sharing in different modes: reading aloud, displaying, duplicating.

Such an implied model underlies most of what follows about planning, getting started, the composing process and receiving the writing.

Planning and the context of writing

It is obvious that writing is affected by the different contexts in which it is done: the physical aspects of the room, the programme of work of which it is part, the relationships with other pupils and with the teacher, the acquired sense of expectations, even the paper or book in which the writing is to be done and the pen or pencil which is being used. In the wider sense, the context includes not just the classroom, but the school itself, the community in which it is set and the homes from which the pupils come, all of which affect their expectations of the writing they are to do.

In fact, though, we know surprisingly little even about the influence of the setting and the medium on the way in which children write. Talking with them reveals that some prefer to write alone at home and some at school among other children; some prefer a silent atmosphere and others a background of music; some like to write straight through at a sitting whereas others like to break up the process with intervals of talking or moving about. The most frequent complaints about having to write in school are 'being pressed for time', 'the noise around you which can put your concentration off', 'having to be quiet for an hour or more', 'teachers looking over your shoulder', or more vaguely, 'the atmosphere in the classroom'. Perhaps the most helpful remark was from a second-year girl who said simply, 'When we're happy we write better.' Unfortunately, our awareness that children do have these different preferences is not accompanied by any certainty that some of the chosen conditions produce *better* writing. Teachers often assume that work done in a busy living room with the television on will be worse than work done peacefully at a quiet desk, but there is no secure evidence for this.

Our teaching and their learning are clearly affected by the classroom in which we work together – what researchers are now calling 'behavioural ecology'. Is a class always taught in the same room? (If not, displaying work and continuity of group projects both become much more difficult, and the teacher is forced into the role of commercial traveller, lugging his case of materials everywhere.) Is that room part of an English suite, with the opportunities that offers for combining groups and team teaching? Does it have its own stockroom, which means that new resources can be deployed if the lesson plan has to be changed? Is there enough space for varied activities to go on simultaneously without the children disturbing each other? How 'fixed' is the furniture? (There are still schools where moving the chairs is frowned on or even forbidden.) A room with desks in neat pairs facing the teacher's desk at the front implies a different pattern of work from one where the chairs are in half-a-dozen groups around tables. One Birmingham teacher with a rather difficult group claimed to have had good results by placing tables round the walls and chairs in the centre of the room. Children sat in a circle for listening to stories or poems and being given instructions, moved the chairs into groups for discussion, and sat at the tables, facing blank walls, for writing. Different arrangements suit different teaching styles, but not all class-rooms are equipped with furniture that can be so flexibly reorganized.

What sort of classroom environment is desirable? In glib, general terms it is one that encourages a desire to write and that provides the means for developing writing abilities. More specifically, this means a room in which a great deal of writing is obvious and available: work by pupils of different ages, pages from magazines, letters, announcements and advertise-

ments on the walls; books, newspapers, periodicals, cata-
logues and brochures on the shelves; folders and box-files of
cuttings, stories, leaflets, guides and manuals on particular
topics. It also means a room in which writing is seen as
bursting out of the bounds of the exercise book, a room that is
equipped not only with paper of different sizes, but with
staplers, scissors, sticky tape, index cards, coloured pens,
carbon paper, drawing pins, paper clips, manilla folders (and,
if possible, with a spirit duplicator). It has to be a room, that
is, in which writing constantly goes on and is seen to go on.

In an ideal world, writing would be much easier if the
demands made back in the 1960s for English to be housed in a
suite of rooms were to be heeded. Flexibility of use makes it
possible for some children to withdraw quietly and to work in
carrels in a study room while others are elsewhere still
discussing their ideas or trying out work by reading it aloud.
It means that groups of children can be in a workshop room
mounting their writing and pictures for display or duplicating
a set of their poems for friends to read, while other groups are
working with the teacher on specific writing difficulties or are
being guided to appropriate materials in the resources collection. Appropriate accommodation makes possible the practice of writing as a collaborative and sharing activity, with the
inevitable accompanying noise and movement, in a way that
is extremely difficult in the conventional classroom with other
subjects being taught on the other side of the wall.

We are also uncertain whether children's preferences in
writing implements are related to the standard of work they
produce. Younger secondary children frequently complain
that they are forced to use fountain pens, which they find
messy, hard to maintain and expensive. I am not aware of any
evidence, though, that they actually write better in the ball-
point pens which many of them prefer. An investigation into
children's use of lined and unlined paper found that the
writing on lined paper was more legible, but that it was
unclear whether or not the lined paper hindered or aided

creativity.[13] Typewriters and word processors are not yet common in English classrooms, but North American colleagues suggest that they will be increasingly used. Limited experience with students who work directly on to a typewriter suggests that one difference from writing in ink is that fewer corrections are made and, possibly, that there are more pauses for thought. It may be that the adding of a visual element to a typewriter keyboard, as in a word processor, may affect this, especially as correction and editing become relatively easy without spoiling the appearance of the text.

Our chief concern, though, must be with the way in which the teacher constructs a particular environment for writing. Here are very brief descriptions of five actual lessons. What differences mark them off from one another?

A A student asks a class to listen to some music, with eyes closed if they wish. They are to see what images, events and ideas the music conjures up in their minds. At the end of a first hearing, some of them are invited to give examples of what they visualized and some of these (the 'approved' ones) are put on the board. The children are then asked to write down their impressions while the music is played for a second time.

B The pupils are in the early stages of several weeks' work on 'Fear'. They have been shown a series of slides representing objects or experiences which may arouse fear (spiders and snakes, having an injection, dropping by parachute etc) and they have discussed their own reactions to these. The teacher reads the 'rat' episode from 1984, and asks the children to consider what would be the most frightening thing with which they could be threatened. They then write about that experience in such a way as to convey to a reader the sense of panic which they feel.

C Pupils have been reading *The Machine Gunners* with their teacher, and now they have divided into groups which have chosen different written outcomes. One group is writing a radio play based on the climax which will later be recorded. Another is planning a newspaper to describe the events and to carry interviews with the different participants. A third is organizing a display of pictures and accompanying articles about the 1939–45 war, and others are similarly engaged in group projects.

D The teacher has produced a box of ideas for writing. Some of these are selected from commercially-produced sources (Abbs's *Broadsheets* and *The Writing Workshop*) and others he has devised himself. Students are encouraged to browse among these and to select freely one which they will use as the basis for their writing. The teacher goes round the class discussing their choices, making suggestions and dealing with difficulties.

E The room is set up as a workshop, with books, art materials, records and cassettes, pictures, magazines, resource kits. The teacher talks informally to individuals and groups. Some of them are clear about what they want to do, some are still uncertain, browsing and chatting. When a student announces that he would like to work on a particular topic, the teacher discusses this with him and points him to possible materials that might be useful.

Without at this point evaluating these lessons comparatively, it can immediately be seen that the writing done in each is affected by the different organizational patterns:

i) The time scale. (A) is a single, one-off lesson, unrelated to work undertaken before or after. (B) and (C) are part of an extended period of work, (D) and (E) employ an approach which continues throughout the year.

ii) The use of resources. In (A) the teacher produces what is needed for that lesson, in (B) and (C) the materials build up during the period spent on the topic and may include items brought by the pupils as well as by the teacher, whereas in (D) and still more in (E) the emphasis is on a wider, multi-purpose and multi-level range of resources, with the implication that all the work will be done in the same classroom: the classroom as workshop.

iii) Establishing the topic. In (A) and (B) the teachers planned that all pupils in the group would write on the same subject, in (C) there is a pre-determined choice of subjects, in (D) there is a much wider range of choice, though still from ideas chosen by the teacher, whereas in (E) there is the assumption that pupils themselves may initiate the topic and that the teacher may respond to this.

iv) Patterns of interaction. In (A) formally and in (D) informally the teacher initiates the work and the pupils are engaged individually on it, in (B) some interchange of ideas and responses between the students is built in, in (C) groups are working collectively and sometimes producing a single written outcome from several people, and in (E) individuals are relating freely with each other and with the teacher.

v) Degree of formality. These five lessons are arranged on a rough scale, with (A) as apparently the most formal and (E) the most informal. (C) and (E) stress co-operative learning, and the teachers appear less dominant, reacting in quite different ways to different groups or individuals in the class.

It is not simply that a teacher elects a particular teaching style and then establishes a corresponding classroom context. Devising a programme of writing for a class is not such a neat theoretical operation. The organizational structure radically affects our relationships with the children we teach and with our colleagues. It has to be hammered out within a whole series of constraints, only some of which can be affected by the individual. For example, a teacher new to a school will have to ask such preliminary questions as these –

i) Is English taught as a self-contained subject, or is it

subsumed within Humanities or Languages or some other overriding Faculty?

ii) Is there team teaching or team planning of work for the whole year?

iii) How far does the Department policy statement or syllabus suggest approaches or topics?

iv) Is there an agreement to concentrate on certain themes during certain terms?

v) Are particular books and resources allocated for your use during a term?

vi) Will all your teaching of a class be in one room, or will you see them in different rooms for different periods?

vii) How are the rooms which you will use laid out and organized?

viii) What are the time constraints? (e.g how long are the periods? single or double? at what time of day? how distributed through the week?)

ix) How available to you are reprographic facilities, audio and video-recorders, display materials etc? How far ahead do they have to be booked?

x) Does the Department carry a stock of successful lesson ideas and outlines, duplicated materials, booklets, and so on, contributed by individuals or worked out by teams of teachers?

Planning and the total English programme

Some of the questions raised at the end of the previous section indicate the problem of relating a group's writing to the overall pattern of English work in the school. When I began teaching, I was instructed to give one period a week to composition, one to poetry, one to grammar, and so on. The activities were seen as unrelated to each other or to the work of other groups in the school. The course books I was expected to use were organized on a similar plan, separating the components of English from each other.

Although this book is specifically about writing, it assumes a model of English as indivisible. Although for convenience a writing programme may be isolated, it can only make sense in relation to all the rest of the work in English. In fact, as will be suggested in chapter 6, particularly in the first three secondary years, writing is generally better presented to children not for its own sake but as a means of doing something else. Writing simply to get better at writing is an unappealing concept.

Within such common structure patterns as blocks of thematic work, or units built around a shared class reader, it will be necessary to check that the writing activities (like those concerned with talk or reading) provide adequate variety, give scope for development and follow an appropriate sequence. These ideas are developed further in pages 74–100. There are different ways of achieving this.

A number of schools plan each year on a simple grid pattern, with selected writing functions (conveying personal experience, fictional story, description of places and people, expressing opinion or argument) along the top and rough developmental 'stages' (usually three or four) down the side. Ideas for written activities on a particular theme can be organized within this framework, which then serves as the basis for a form's work. The first pieces of writing within any of the modes enable the teacher to establish programmes for individuals or groups according to the kind of development that is anticipated or hoped for. Other schools practise versions of what Paul Francis has called 'blob theory'.[14] A mixed-ability class follows a unit of work within which there is a range of written (and other) assignments, represented by black and white blobs. 'The black blobs are the ones all pupils must do, the white blobs are the ones some pupils may do', and the problems are to decide which are the black blobs and who should do which of the white blobs. However careful the forward planning, however, it is ultimately the teacher who has to ensure that any group's work is consistent by asking such questions as these when setting a piece of writing:

Why exactly am I giving this piece of work to this group at this moment?

How does it relate to the total pattern of their work this week? this term? this year? to what they have done in the past and will do in the future?

What kinds of development am I hoping to encourage by this? How shall I assess its success?

How far can the work be adapted to meet the different needs, abilities and interests of individuals in the group?

What new demands does this work make? How shall I need to prepare the students for these?

How far will it encourage them to experiment or to make new discoveries for themselves?

How, precisely, is this work going to be set up? Are my instructions about the audience, the purpose, the goals of the writing quite clear?

The amount of overall freedom within a total plan obviously varies from situation to situation. A whole year's work can be team planned and team taught on such a wide topic as the Elements or the Seasons. A term's unit on the Family may be worked out in tremendous detail, with weekly 'launch' meetings of presentations, films and videotapes, specific lesson-by-lesson specifications for all classes, with long lists of back-up materials and over thirty specific writing suggestions, chosen to give adequate variety. The planning may be embodied in duplicated pupils' booklets (Writing About Ourselves, Friends and Enemies, Looking Forward) which provide necessary materials and organize the writing. Alternatively, a group of teachers may draw up guides for colleagues, based on their own successful work, which suggest varieties of possible approach. By way of examples, here are two such guides intended for use with third years. The first suggests four possible structures for the familiar Desert Island theme and goes on to propose varied writing activities within a wider programme drawing on the 'Frames' in A. W. England's *Islands* pack. The second demonstrates how closely writing is tied in with other activities in a programme of work built around a novel by Frederick Grice.

The Desert Island theme

GENERAL SCHEME

1 The extended story could be the underlying, continuous work while other work is in progress.

   Groups of pupils could be working on different blocks of work, eg, poetry, drama, writing plays etc, and all could come together at the end to present their work to the rest of the class.

2 One of the novels, e.g. *The Boy Who Was Afraid*, *Treasure Island*, *Lord of the Flies* could be read first to act as a stimulus to the following work. Alternatively the novel could be read at the end to draw the work to a conclusion.

3 Improvisation (see Drama Workframes in *Islands* Kit) could be used as the initial stimulus leading to the writing of the extended story.

4 The whole class could decide on the island so that all the work done has a common ground. (Apart from the Extended Desert Island Story.) This would involve deciding on the shape/size/features of the island before starting. The groups of pupils could work on different aspects. Group work cards could be made for each group.

POSSIBLE WORK WITHIN EACH SCHEME

1 *Extended Desert Island story* = use of narrative, descriptive and explanatory writing.

   Stimulated by reading extracts from *Robinson Crusoe* in *Thoughtshapes* and looking at the pictures in the

Islands Kit and/or improvisation. (See Drama Work Frames.)

Chapter I: Arriving on the island: how you arrive (shipwreck/aircrash etc).

Chapter II: Exploring the island: a map.

Chapter III: Setting up home. How to build a house (explaining things) plus diagrams.

Chapter IV: Adventures on the Island.

Chapter V: The final chapter: saved?

It is possible to precede each chapter by reading further extracts to stimulate ideas, e.g. from *Robinson Crusoe, The Boy who was Afraid* (e.g. Chapter 3, *The Island* also in *Islands: The Forbidden Island*). Also one could include the idea of the island being the 'ideal' world to live in, see *Utopia*.

2 *Poetry*

Stimulated by improvisation (see section on drama) readings of selected extracts from any of the stories, pictures and slides from holidays spent on islands. (Majorca, Isle of Wight, the Bahamas!) The poems could describe the island itself, the survivors – their feelings and experiences.

Shape Poetry could be written in the shape of the island, the wildlife, the weather etc.

Ideas for writing poetry are given on Work Frames 1, 14, 20 and 24 in the Islands Kit.

3 *Playwriting*

This could be based on
a) Extracts from stories read, e.g. scenes adapted from *Lord of the Flies, Treasure Island*, etc. Also see Work Frames 1, 16.

continued overleaf

b) Ideas on the drama cards in the *Islands* Kit.

c) If the group or class has decided on an island with certain characteristics a play could be written based on several survivors and their adventures. These could be written independently by each group or alternatively the story of the play could be worked out beforehand and each group of pupils could write one scene. It would then be possible to write a script for a complete play based on the island. These plays could be taped, or presented to the class.

4 *Drama*

See work cards in Islands Kit.
Possible ways of using them

a) *Improvisation*: Dividing the class into 3 groups and giving one card to each group. Alternatively all the class doing the work from one card directed by the teacher. (This may be used as a stimulus for writing.)

b) Working on the play(s) previously written by the groups (see playwriting).

5 *Writing in different styles*

a) *Advertising.* Designing a campaign trying to 'sell' the island as a holiday resort. (See Group Frames 1 and 3.) Including a written guided tour of the island.

b) *Newspaper reporting. Individual work.* Imagine you are a newspaper reporter visiting the island. After interviewing several people send your 'exclusive' report to your newspaper. (Also see Frame 14.) *Group work.* Design the newspaper for the island. A front page cover of all the latest events, weather, explorations and discoveries, adventures, deaths etc.

c) *Writing letters.* A letter to be sent in a bottle to the outside world describing the different hardships, the desire to be saved etc.

Also see Work Frame 6.

6 *Writing for taping*

a) Plays.

b) A journalist interviewing survivors on the island; contrasting interviews with different people about their arrival, their existence on the island, adventures, food, health etc. (See work Frame 14.)

c) *Desert Island radio*! A radio programme devised by the people on the island highlighting different aspects of life on the island: interviews, weather reports, pleas for help, 'desert island discs', a discussion on their needs, and perhaps a more lighthearted one on the one book they would have brought with them, the one tool etc, etc.

7 *Literature work*

a) *Individual reading*. A novel listed in the bibliography. Individual written work could be set on the novel when read.

b) *Group/class reading*. Reading of short stories, extracts, novels. Following work on the stories and extracts in *Islands, an Anthology* is covered excellently on the Work Frame cards. Both individual and group work is given and each card is graded according to the relative difficulty of the work proposed. Many different types of work are given including comprehension, e.g., Work Frames 7 and 8.

8 *Expressing opinions, note-taking and summarizing*

Meetings of the 'islanders' to decide policy, rules, means of escape, trials of people who have broken rules etc. (Extracts from *Lord of the Flies* could be read first.)

continued overleaf

These could be held periodically while the project is in progress and different groups could be responsible for taking minutes and 'publishing' them in the classroom.

9 *Radio-vision programme* (See Group Frame 2.)

   a) Use of slides and an accompanying read or taped commentary about different islands of the world.

   b) Slides taken of the play written by the class with an accompanying narrative or TV documentary account. A programme of work like this would probably last for a month at least, or, if it were going well, half a term.

Bonnie Pit Laddie by F. Grice

1 *As a preliminary to reading the novel*

Reading together descriptions by George Orwell or Clancy Segal of going down a pit, followed by group discussion of questions on the extract. Looking at pictures of early miners and reading their comments in *Things Working* – The English Project. Discovering impressions as a class. Using lists of words and phrases for the sensory impressions of going down a mine to prepare for writing poems. Perhaps suggesting the structure of a contrast between the open air and underground.

2 *Reading the novel*

As the book divides itself naturally into a series of episodes in Dick's life, I read it to the class as a series of instalments, with confident readers taking the parts of Dick and his family. At appropriate points I would stop for several lessons for some of the following activities.

a) Working out the 'layout' of Branton; drawing maps and marking on them places from the novel.

b) Improvisations – acting out, e.g. a confrontation between Mr Sleath and angry miners and wives; the eviction of strikers from their homes.

c) Writing a newspaper report of the strike.

d) Writing a story called *First day down the pit*, perhaps from Dick's point of view using ideas from the novel and from earlier discussions and reading.

e) Improvisation using different situations but a similar theme – groups working on 'First day at work'.

f) Using information from the novel and from the library or geography lessons, working out in pairs how coal was mined at the time of the story and what different jobs the miners did. Comparing this with modern mining. Pairs then explaining to the rest of the class what they have discovered.

3 *After reading the novel*

a) Preparing and performing a television programme about 'The Branton Affair', modelled on *Panorama* and *Man Alive* investigations. Groups of 4 or 5 work on the following:

  i) Commentators introducing the village, the pit, and the management problem. Explaining how the strike and the accident came about.

  ii) Angry wives interviewed in their back yards.

  iii) A reporter at the head of the 'escape' staple interviewing exhausted miners as they struggle out.

  iv) A confrontation in the studio between Mr Sleath, and trade union officials. The groups come together after a lesson of preparation.

b) A choice of written work related to the novel.

continued overleaf

i) Imagine that you are Mr Sleath. Pick one incident from the novel and give your account of it, being careful to explain how you felt.

ii) Imagine that you are Dick and give your account of the day of the accident.

iii) Write portraits of Dick and his family and of other important characters in the story.

This block of work would probably last for four or five weeks.

Planning and development

Any planning of a writing programme has to depend on teachers' views of what children's writing is typically 'like' at ages 11, 13 or 15, of the more obvious marks of improvement that they show, or of the steps by which they progressively move towards maturity of expression. In other words, we depend on a theory of development. Unfortunately, getting better at writing is not a simple, uncomplicated concept, and we do not have many trustworthy maps to guide us. Surprisingly little work has been done on the way in which children slowly progress from the ability to write single words to connected sentences and then a brief narrative, and so on. It appears that progress is made in irregular spurts[15] but we know little about the ways in which our teaching affects that progress.

Teachers of older children hardly need reminding that there are limits to the modification they can expect to bring about in the pupils' writing. In a sense, almost all of them *can* write. According to the APU more than 96 percent of 11-year-olds have sufficient control of writing, spelling and punctuation to make what they write understandable at a first reading.[16] On the other hand, the range of abilities with which teachers have to contend is continually widening with age. Compare the

first pieces of work done by two children in their new middle
school, asked to write about themselves.

Myself

I am ten years old in October. I go to ＿＿＿＿＿ Junior High
School. I like playing rounders. At my old school I was
champion speller. I'm called ＿＿＿＿＿. My best friend is
Alison ＿＿＿＿＿. My old school is called ＿＿＿＿＿ Primary
School. When I grow up I would like to be a policewoman.
I'am intrested in sewing. My favorite programme is Starsky
and Hutch.

Myself

I went to speddway. I went for an Hot dog. I sat down to
wacht Speedway till it finished, went home.

The first of these nine-year-olds was rated by her teachers
among the best three in her year, the second in the weakest
three. There are certainly indications of a difference in ability:
the first writes considerably more, gives a wider range of
information, can use a subordinate clause and is aware of the
apostrophe even though she cannot use it accurately. However, there are also similarities between the two. The first
writes largely in the same monotonous simple sentences as the
second, is perhaps even more random in the ordering of
information, lacks any sense of structure (whereas the second
shows some elementary sense of closure), and uses the same
sort of expressive voice. These children are still inhabiting
what is essentially the same linguistic world. Move on four
years, and consider the representative strongest and weakest
pupils early in their final year at the middle school, set to write
about a frightening night-time experience.

My Most Frightening Experience

I had been staying with relations who lived in a lonely
farmhouse on the Yorkshire moors. My relations had been
called away suddenly and I was left alone. The wind was

howling round the house and down the chimney. It was snowing, that meant my relations would be late back because the road would be blocked. Perhaps they wouldn't come back at all tonight, perhaps they had had an accident. No, I was just letting my imagination get the better of me. How I hated the dark lonely farmhouse. All the shadows the flickering fire, made me feel nervous, there was a deathly fear gripping my heart.

All of a sudden there was a strong gust of wind which blew down the chimney, and the fire went out. I sat there for a few minutes shivering, then I put some more logs on the fire. I lay back on the chair, and fell asleep. I was awakened by the sound of footsteps coming up the gravel path. I let my imagination run away with me again, maybe it was a burglar or a murderer. I grabbed the poker and stood behind the door. The door creaked open very slowly, I held my breath a dark figure walked in, I lifted the poker and hit the figure over the head, he collapsed on the floor. Then, quickly I turned on the light, and there, on the floor was my cousin. I found out the next morning, (when he was conscious again) that he had come back to stay with me because it was such an awful night, and he knew how much I hated being alone. That was the last time I let my imagination get the better of me again.

A Bump int he Nig

Wnos I hAd a Bump in the Night I was shivering I got hot ov bed I poot my sllips on I oppd the dor wert doon the strs it wos the MooMy gon shot Shot it it was bliieding it wot ded it froo a chre at my it mst my it wert froo the wid and I jupt on the barck.

Here there are few similarities. The first tells a coherent, structured story, the second a jumbled, incomplete string of incidents. The first chooses an appropriate style and narrative conventions for building up excitement and simultaneously creating the sense of conflict between illusion and reality, whereas the second uses the same undifferentiated style as for all other writings. The first uses fluent variation of sentence structure; the second monotonous brief simple sentences, unseparated by any punctuation. The first shows a sense of causality and possibility (that meant, perhaps, because) which is wholly lacking in the second. The language of the first is largely free from major errors, whereas the second is full of mistakes.

An awkward question arises from this. If we claim that our teaching is responsible for, or at least has aided, the development shown by more able pupils between 9 and 13, do we also accept our share of responsibility for the comparative failure of the less able and less motivated to progress? Because most of our students get better at writing, we assume that we are teaching them effectively, but how much of their improvement simply results from the fact that they are growing older and more experienced? Our attention has been called to the way in which some pupils' writing regresses when they go to a new school or change classes, and to the fact that some can write coherently out of school but only fragmentarily in lessons.[17] When Harold Rosen investigated the writing of fifty pupils throughout their O-level year to discover how much they improved in that time, his answer was 'mostly they don't, they deteriorate' (though he was careful to consider the limitations of the enquiry).[18]

The necessary idealism about our teaching strategies may need to be balanced by a healthy questioning of their effectiveness.

What is it, in any case, that we mean by talking of 'improvement' or 'increased maturity' or 'development'? Andrew Wilkinson describes it concisely as a 'movement from dependence to autonomy; from convention to uniqueness; from unconsciousness to awareness; from subjectivity to objectivity; from ignorance to understanding; from self to neighbour as self'.[19]

At the specifically linguistic level there has been much research, but it is of limited help to teachers planning programmes. There is a certain obviousness about such findings as that, on the whole, older children write at greater length than younger ones, have wider vocabularies and use more complex sentences. The continuing work of Kathleen Perera and others, which suggests that in general there is a discernible sequence in which children acquire the ability to use different forms of subordinate clause, say, may prove to be more significant. The real difficulty is how to translate observations of linguistic maturity into strategies that will aid it. When students were asked to consolidate numbers of simple sentences into fewer units, Kellogg W. Hunt found that the older they were the greater the number of sentences they could combine into one, the more syntactical changes they made, the less use of co-ordinating conjunctions and the more use of apposition they employed. His conclusion was that 'a sentence-combining curriculum' enhanced 'syntactic maturity', as measured in this way.[20] Well, of course. Teaching students to combine sentences is likely to improve their ability at combining sentences, but what has not yet been convincingly demonstrated is that this improves their free writing.

It may be more helpful to consult recent studies which consider how children perceive written tasks and attempt to carry them out at different stages of maturity. The developmental sequences suggested by Wilkinson and others, or by Dixon and Stratta,[21] illustrated as they are by examples of children's work, serve not only for assessment but for planning. The links between emotional, linguistic, cognitive and stylistic development can help teachers to sharpen their awareness of the kinds of activity appropriate to assist that development.

They can help themselves and each other by simple longitudinal studies of the work in their own schools. Selecting a particular kind of assignment (description of a person, or arguing a case, or reporting an event) they can compare work by average, able and less able children in different years writing on that topic. If it is available, they can consider the writing done by a single pupil over a number of years and examine the ways in which development is discernible. Here, for example, is a brief study of the first short stories written in each of years 1–5 by one able girl.

In her first September at a new secondary school, Joanna wrote a story called 'An Overdose of the Potion' which filled over five pages of her exercise book. Told in the first person, it describes how a schoolgirl finds a spell for making people smaller, gives a dose to a schoolfellow, Eleanor Spike, who thinks she is too tall, but reduces her too far and has to apply the antidote to restore her. Even as a fantasy it is full of inconsistencies and implausibilities. How is it that nobody has ever discovered the ancient recipe in a school library book? Would Eleanor be likely to drink the potion? Why did Eleanor's mother do nothing about her daughter's apparent disappearance for several days? If Eleanor is only one inch high, how can she drink the antidote from a thimble? The cartoon-like style and the moralizing tone, which implies condemnation of Eleanor but not of the interfering narrator, are very like Enid Blyton's. The story is a string of incidents, put together fluently but with no real sense of interaction between the characters. The opening lines show the monotony of the emphasis on the narrator's actions: I went, I was looking, I picked up, I put it back, I was reading, I turned, I looked...

> It started when I went to the library to choose a book. I was looking through the pages when something fell out and fluttered to the floor. I picked it up and put it back without looking at it.
>
> I did not think of it again until one night, while I was reading the book I turned to the page where I had put it. I looked at it closely this time.

There are plenty of indications, however, that Joanna is

potentially a very able writer. Not only is this a lengthy piece relatively free from mechanical errors, it is also appropriately structured, with a crisp beginning and a firm ending ('Even now she ignores me but I always think of her strange secret'). It is clear that Joanna knows how stories work. She enjoys evocative words: the spell is written 'in thin, spidery, slanting handwriting on a sheet of paper that was yellow with age'. She can handle subordinate clauses of time with confidence, and occasionally attempts more complex constructions. There is a general sense that she is 'hearing' what she writes.

A year later, Joanna is attempting a naturalistic slice-of-life. The central character, Sharon, is still a schoolgirl like herself, but the interaction with her friend, her mother and the headmaster is much more convincingly represented, and much of the story is told through words put into their mouths, which realize them to some degree as characters. The protagonist is seen from the outside, not presented in the first person. There is more concern for feelings and attitudes, and developing awareness of people's concern about how they appear to others. When she is summoned to see the headmaster, Mrs Green puts on her best coat and hat, because 'She wanted Mr Fields to get a good impression of her, even if he were not pleased with Sharon'; when she talks to him, it is with 'an effort to use the same calm tones as the headmaster'; she leaves him 'using all the charm she could muster'. Compare the opening of this story with the one a year earlier.

> Sharon Green walked through the school gates, and slumped down on one of the steps. She was not in a good mood, and she felt tired. She waited impatiently for her friend, Louise Hammond to arrive, but did not see her when she came.
>
> 'Hi, Sharon! Sharon!' she called. Sharon got up reluctantly and went to meet her.
>
> 'Hi Louise.'
>
> 'Did you see that film last night?'

'Which film?'

'There was only one on last night. That one called "Lost".'

'It was rubbish. I've seen it before, anyway.'

'Hey, let's have a skeg at your Maths homework. I only did half of mine.'

Sharon gave her the book. She felt brightened by Louise's high spirits.

Development is less obvious in a purely linguistic sense than in the changing assumptions about what story-telling involves. The characters are distinguished by their speech styles; the episode does not depend on a heavily manipulated plot; it is assumed that readers will recognize the 'truth' of what happens.

In September of the third year, in a story called 'The Rains Came Down', Joanna has moved outside the world of school. Her characters are an old man, his married daughter and his five-year-old grandson (so would grandpa really be *so* old?). There is a conscious attempt to shape the story significantly. Despite the mother's hesitation, grandfather takes Peter for a walk in the rain. They share observations of nature – ink-caps and spiders – but the old man is taken ill and passes out. A policeman finds them together and the old man, protesting, is bundled off to hospital. The point is made implicitly rather than being directly stated. Joanna is now working (almost certainly unconsciously) at new technical problems: how much explanation of motives is necessary? How can feelings and attitudes be indicated without naming them? She has realized that it is not always necessary to name and describe characters at the moment they first appear. Here the characters are referred to almost all the time as the old man, the boy, the mother, as though to universalize the family tensions. We only learn the names as they use them. The story begins:

The old man sat still in his chair staring at the window down which the rain was pouring. It had been raining almost solidly for five days, and only his daughter had been out of the house. At his feet the child was sitting restlessly, fiddling with a piece of the railway track he had been playing with. He was five, and, the old man reflected, when he was that age they had lived in the country and he had gone out every day, so that he never sat restlessly as the boy was doing now.

'Margaret', he called. The child turned as his mother came into the room.

'What is it, Dad?' she asked.

'Could Peter and I go for a walk? He's never seen the country as I have, and I'd like to see it again.'

'But Dad, it's raining', she said patiently.

'I know (she) it is. But we have been inside for five days and the child is growing restless.'

'Oh, all right then,' she replied, 'but make sure you wrap up well and come back in plenty of time for tea.'

Joanna's stories have tended to become more economical. 'The Rain Came Down' is rather shorter than 'An Overdose of the Potion', two years before. Early in the fourth year, she attempted a story which condensed the essential action into a single brief incident. It returns to the world of familiar experience: a girl introducing a friend from a different social background to her own family. Although the story is written in the first person, the narrator plays only a small part in the direct action; the real subject is her shifting responses, her embarrassment, anxiety and pity at what the others do and say. The point of the story is the way in which the story-teller has to reassess her friend and their relationship. The climax comes when the apparently poised Charlotte, who has graciously offered to help with the washing-up, has an accident.

Charlotte had dropped one of the plates from our best tea-service and was looking down at it helplessly.

'I'm very sorry', she said at length.

'That's alright', replied my mother. 'It was an accident, that's all.' She began to clear up the pieces. Charlotte continued to look embarrassed.

'I'll pay you for it', she said, no longer the sophisticated young lady, but a school girl desperately trying to make it up. My mother evidently thought that she was too worried about it, that it was only a little thing, and tried to cheer her up. But Charlotte was miserable because she felt guilty about the plate and coming into a family where she was obviously someone quite different, and caused so much awkwardness. In a very short while she suggested that it was time she should go home.

She said goodbye and thank you to my mother, who was trying to conceal her relief, in a shaken copy of the smooth clear voice she had used on arriving. I walked to the end of the road with her in silence, and we parted quickly. I returned to the house also relieved, but puzzled, as I had expected it all to be easy, and to have made us even better friends than before.

In September of the fifth year, in a prose sketch called 'Waiting', Joanna gets inside the fictional life of Cathy, a lonely girl who has left home to work in London.

Cathy leant her back against the barrier and frowned. Why was the bus always so late? Why did she bother to queue, day in, day out? Why was she going home at all?

Cathy had left home to live and work in London. She had rented a small bed-sit and managed to get herself a job. But that was a month ago. In a month the huge city had swallowed her, made her a nobody, like a grain of sand on a beach. There was no-one in the whole city she could speak of as a friend, and no-one whose eyes would light up in recognition if her name was mentioned.

The whole story is managed within a few minutes during which Cathy queues for a bus. The rest is told in flashbacks –

the short-lived kindness of other girls in the office when she first took the job, an invitation to a disco – cut in with awareness of the people and the conversations around her in the queue. Essentially the story is an analysis of Cathy, her wishes, fears and daydreams. 'She felt that the city was drying up her personality.'

Over a period of four years, Joanna has developed considerably as a writer of stories. The processes involved are too complex to be conveyed adequately by selective reference and quotation, but at the risk of distorting by generalizing, her work seems to show such changes as these:

i)   from a naive view of story as a series of events to a more sophisticated sense of story grounded in what happens within an individual in certain situations;

ii) from a sequential, linear plot to a concentration on key moments in which necessary information is conveyed indirectly or by flash-back;

iii) from reliance on familiar surroundings and people to a willingness to create an imaginary world that is coherent and believable;

iv) from a patchy awareness of the reader, and what that reader will accept as credible, to a conscious providing and sequencing of information necessary to comprehend the story;

v)   from simple to more complex moral judgements, conveyed through the whole action rather than being tacked on;

vi) from an inconsequential emotional tone and a sometimes inappropriate style to the deliberate conveying of an appropriate mood through a consistent style;

vii) from direct involvement as a person in the story to 'becoming' another character and then to withdrawal from the action to concentrate wholly on others;

viii) from seeing other characters as two-dimensional puppets to an awareness of them as individuals with their own histories, problems and wishes;

ix) from describing people's characteristics to letting them reveal themselves, in action and in dialogue, and then particularly through interaction.

What has changed basically is Joanna's view of what being 'a writer of stories' means.

Planning and sequence

The Schools Council Working Paper No. 62, *English in the 1980s*, suggested among its concerns for the future 'Understanding ways of weaving the elements of English into a continuous sequence of lessons'. The language is understandably vague, but the sense is clear. Without the supporting (or cramping) structure of a course book, how do we give coherence to the programme?

Despite all the efforts of orderly syllabuses, nobody has yet succeeded in devising an overall, sequential model for the teaching of writing, a neat hierarchy of skills in which A leads to B and then to C. This is not to say that there are no learning sequences, that some activities should not normally precede others, but simply that – unlike mathematics – writing cannot be taught by isolating single elements and building them up one on another. Learning to write involves developing a series of interdependent abilities simultaneously. Think of being called on to handle dialogue in a narrative. If you have had no experience of doing this, then the whole idea of 'dialogue' will be hard to imagine. You may be told that you cannot write it down 'properly' without learning about speech marks. Learning about speech marks makes no sense until you know what is meant by recording conversation. You cannot record invented conversation until you have the ability to 'hear' other voices than your own and put them on paper. To put them on paper means being able to use speech marks, and so on. To advance in writing, mechanical skills, particular 'crafts' of language are locked together with personal developments in awareness and sensitivity. The teacher can focus on a particular aspect, can highlight it for the pupils, but writing assignments involve working globally on a number of frontiers at once.

One of the reasons that students sometimes get discouraged is that we encourage them to think that planning can achieve too much. A carefully prepared lesson goes badly and one done off-the-cuff succeeds. All of us have the experience of having to reorganize work because of unforeseen circumstances: we lose our voices, half the class has to go for medical inspection, workmen's drills in the next room make talk impossible, somebody has removed the tape-recorder or film-projector which was essential for the lesson. Worst of all, we suddenly discover that we cannot go on to the next stage because the children's writing reveals that they are not ready for it.

The Secondary Committee of NATE carried out an investigation, entitled *The Best-Laid Plans*, into the ways in which teachers had to modify their intentions for a class's work over a period of about half a term. The overwhelming impression from the diaries kept by a number of teachers was of constant adjustments to plans, coping with emergencies, reassessing and reordering materials, deciding to follow new lines. Flexibility of this kind is hard for a student, who tends either to follow the planned lesson grimly, regardless of what happens, or to abandon it altogether. Perhaps we pay too little attention to the skills of resourcefulness, of thinking on the feet, or restructuring within an overall framework, since these are certainly going to be vital in school.

The most general planning principle of experienced English teachers is one of progressive narrowing down. Long-range goals for a year are narrowed to immediate goals for a particular lesson; from a broad list of activities for the term, some are selected for a week or a fortnight, and then one is chosen for lesson two on Friday; feedback from the pupils and their work is used to suggest which particular ability out of a considerable number will be highlighted for attention next.

Considering writing in particular – while acknowledging that, as the Working Paper indicates, it must never be isolated from other English activities – it is clear that *sequence* can be established in different overlapping ways, all of them important.

SEQUENCE OF DEVELOPMENT

The importance of planning in terms of the observed ways in which children seem to develop writing abilities has been discussed on pages 74*ff*. It may also be helpful to make children themselves more aware of such sequences. Leslie Stratta has told me of a teacher who gave his pupils a set of compositions representing 'staging posts', told them to identify the one that came closest to their own work and then got them to diagnose by looking at the next one in what particular respects they thought their writing needed to improve.

SEQUENCE OF WRITING ACTIVITIES

Many traditional schemes of work and syllabuses (including one I drafted myself in the 1950s) suggested lists of different writing activities for each school year organized beneath headings like 'narrative', 'descriptive', 'argumentative' under the well-meaning if rather hazy impression that there was a natural learning sequence for each. In one Nottingham school, for example, six kinds of written activity were distinguished, and suggestions were given for appropriate work in each of these for the first four years of the school. Among the proposed activities were these:

Description

Year 1 Descriptions from life of local scenes, buildings, people and objects (stressing importance of accurate observation).

2 Descriptions of people, places, events from pictures (emphasis on conveying sense impressions in words, selecting viewpoint or aspect).

3 Emotionally-loaded descriptions from different viewpoints. Descriptions of people to include personality.

4 Setting descriptions in time and place. Use of changing viewpoint. Characters revealed in action and through dialogue.

Letters

Year 1 Informal letters to friends (real, where possible). Simple letters of thanks and requests.

2 Asking for information. Purchasing goods.

3 More formal letters, accepting and refusing invitations. Simple business letters.

4 More formal business letters: applications for jobs, etc. 'Tone' letters of complaint, sympathy, apology.

Extended and group activities

Year 1 Group magazines. 'Island' books. Personal journals and diaries.

2 Group serial stories. Wall newspapers. Autobiographies, in several chapters. Enquiries within the class.

3 Form magazine. Interviews within the school as basis for articles. Collections of reviews (books, plays, films, TV programmes). Local guide book.

4 Form short story anthology. Interviewing and reporting (out of school). Group plays or film-scripts.

Such a scheme is based on the teacher's perception of natural learning sequence. In the example given, for instance, it is assumed that describing an actual, familiar person is easier than (or is a necessary preparation for) describing someone from a picture, that the style for 'thank-you' letters is to be acquired well before the style for writing apologies, that at the personal level keeping a journal of immediate events precedes the retrospection necessary for autobiography. Some of the assumptions now look much more dubious than others. At least such a system had the advantage of providing a neat looking writing programme, and avoided cries of 'But we did this last year!' It did understand that a range of different writing activities should be going on in each year of the school. It avoided the over-controlled step-by-step approach of course books of the same period, one of which outlined the composition work for the whole of the first year as follows:

1 Narrative paragraphs
2 Narrative paragraphs
3 Narrative paragraphs
4 Descriptive paragraphs
5 Descriptive paragraphs
6 Explaining how to do things
7 Use of a topic sentence
8 Letter-writing
9 Making a narrative summary
10 Business letters
11 More summarizing
12 Argument
13 Revision exercises
14 Revision exercises
15 Revision exercises
16 Revision exercises
17 Revision exercises
18 Revision exercises[22]

Nevertheless, there are two good reasons why most schools seemed to abandon the formal syllabus of year-by-year activities of the kind cited. First, such a programme tends to reduce writing to a rather artificial series of exercises. Those of us who have tried it found that the imposed sequence did not always, in fact, fit the order in which many children needed to learn to write. Also, even within a relatively restricted ability range, there were always pupils who were not ready for (or who were well beyond) the activities suggested for their year. Second, there have to be doubts about the validity of claiming that the different 'kinds of discourse' are not only distinct but also require different, appropriate written styles. Teachers are aware that much children's writing is equally in a number of these modes at once. A first-year child, writing on 'Pets I Enjoy Keeping', moves in and out of narrative, description, information-giving and argument within the discursive framework. It is not possible to categorize her lively work as a story or an essay or a piece of exposition. The same is frequently true of the way in which children write about their visits to places of interest. There is little point in building a programme on a model which does not actually fit what children produce.

Abandoning the syllabus, though, produced its own crop of problems. Inexperienced teachers were left without any guide of what was seen as appropriate for children of different ages. There was a temptation to go for effective one-off lessons instead of trying to fit them into a developmental pattern. Popular topics tended to come up year after year ('This is the third time I've done War!'). Without being so rigid that flexibility disappears, it should be possible for members of a department to establish some sequence of what Moffett calls 'a proper learning order', suggesting that some tasks are seen as more complex and difficult than others. The Nottingham syllabus quoted here was probably right in suggesting that describing a character through the eyes of other people should come after descriptions from the writer's own viewpoint and before attempting the self-revelation of an imagined character in dialogue. Writing stories to follow an introductory sentence (I shall never forget the look on his face ...) would seem logically to precede writing stories to arrive at a given conclusion (... I shall always be grateful to my grandfather's braces), and both would come before the more difficult task of writing the central section of a story between the given introductory and concluding paragraphs. Without chopping up the sequences arbitrarily into year-long units, it should be possible to devise patterns of work that assist progress in different written forms. The Bullock Report was surely right in its conviction: 'We believe that progress in writing through-out the school years should be marked by an increasing differentiation in the kinds of writing a pupil can successfully tackle.'(11.8)

Not only are certain written modes more inherently difficult than others, all of them also involve abilities at different levels, which may or may not be adequately developed by individual learners. It certainly seems true, for instance, that one of the reasons that 15-year-olds enjoy argumentative writing much less than more 'imaginative' topics[23] is that the mode appears difficult because it demands skills which are not fully understood and which they have not been helped to develop. Argument is not a simple, global concept. Leslie Stratta and John Dixon have begun to disentangle some of the necessary distinctions that need to be made about argumentative topics, for example:

i) between the need to explore ideas and the wish to reach a conclusion;
ii) between the partisan advocacy of a position and the dispassionate exploration of an issue;
iii) between the case grounded solely on personal experience and the one generalizing from public knowledge;
iv) between the intention of modifying behaviour and of affecting opinions or beliefs.

The authors have gone on from this to argue for an appropriate sequence of work in English, in which individuals will be helped 'to move from simpler to more complex functions for Argument, and from easier to more difficult forms of writing'.[24] Other similar patterns of movement might be from immediate experience through recollection of the past towards anticipation and generalization, or from the self-directed egocentric monologue towards a wide range of other-directed audiences and modes, or from the particular and explicit to the general and implicit.

Instead of the traditional syllabus of work to be covered, one senior high school in Hull has drawn up a list of writing activities thought by the staff to be appropriate for a given year. New teachers can be helped by seeing in this way what more experienced colleagues are doing. Twelve different 'kinds of writing' are identified for the third year, including descriptive, explaining things, expressing opinions, writing letters and so on. Here as a sample are some of the suggestions made for work under three of these headings.

Personal narrative

a) Writing in which pupils recreate and give form to their own experience.

b) Accounts of particular events and experiences.

Experiences at school, e.g. The first day at school; Being caught and punished for doing something wrong; accounts of appearing in concerts, football teams, etc. Family experiences, e.g. weddings, deaths, new brothers and sisters, Christmas, holidays, etc. Individual experiences, e.g. incidents connected with hobbies; frightening, happy, sad, embarrassing, exciting, dangerous experiences; friendships; enemies, etc. Connected and extended accounts of the past, making biographies.

c) Group and class discussion, remembering and sharing experience before writing about it.

Stimulus from reading, e.g. descriptions of the first day at school by Laurie Lee and William Saroyan in

First Day, punishment in school – the pandybatting incident from *A Portrait of the Artist as a Young Man* by James Joyce, collecting tadpoles described in *Kes* by Barry Hines, etc. (There are several other suggestions in the department's *Theme Work* document.)

Approaches to beginning and organizing the writing of autobiographies are described in the *Theme Work* document.

Narrative – story

a) The creation of imagined characters and situations and the structuring of these into different narrative forms.

b) Suspense stories, e.g. *Escape*! Episodic stories, e.g. *Desert Island Story, The Story of a Journey*. Humorous stories, e.g. *Imagine you are invisible for a day, tell the story of what happens*. Stories ending in anti-climax, e.g. a story involving disappointment after excited preparations. Stories blending dreams with reality, e.g. *Write your version of a day in Ernie's life*. Stories with surprise endings, e.g. *Write a story about someone who becomes a very unlikely hero*, etc.

c) Using stories read with the class as inspiration and 'pattern' for the pupil's own narratives: Suspense stories – extracts involving Tom and Huck in the graveyard, Jim Hawkins in the apple barrel or the hero of *Moonfleet* hiding in the crypt, *The Tree* by W. C. Badcock, *Power* by Jack Cope, *Through the Tunnel* by Doris Lessing, *Mr Corbett's Ghost* by Leon Garfield. Episodic stories – longer stories or novels like *The Hobbit, Robinson Crusoe*. Humorous stories – *The Champion of the World* by Roald Dahl, *The Christmas Party* by George Layton. *The Murderer* by Ray Bradbury. Stories with anti-climaxes – *The Holiday* by George Layton, *The Pigman* by John Wain. Dream and

continued overleaf

reality stories – *Ernie and his Incredible Illucinations* by Alan Ayckbourn. Stories with surprise endings – *The Goalkeeper's Revenge* by Bill Naughton, *The Balaclava Story* by George Layton, *In the Forest of the Night* in *Imagine*.

Using pictures suggesting situations and/or characters for stories, e.g. in *Things Being Various, Story Board, Impact 1 and 2*.

Using a combination of starters, e.g. see *Section Three* for ways of starting a desert island story.

Using characters from stories, novels and plays in different situations, e.g. putting Claud and Gordon from *The Champion of the World* into another improbable 'master-plan', using George Hooping and his friends from *Extraordinary Little Cough* by Dylan Thomas.

Expressing opinions

a) In the third year only a few pupils are able to form opinions and express them in writing. Therefore it is important (*i*) that writing is preceded by some kind of discussion (see *Kinds of Talking*), and (*ii*) that subjects are chosen which are close to the pupils' interests and experience.

b) Essays expressing the pupils' own opinion; speeches expressing a point of view as part of a debate, trial, etc.; articles or statements of opinion written in the role of a character taking part in a trial, or hearing.

c) Some topics which have been successful with third years: *cruelty to animals*, prepared by group and class discussion, perhaps started off by groups listing different kinds of cruelty, written work title 'What do you think about the ways in which men treat animals?'; *the existence of ghosts and the supernatural*, accounts of ghosts, etc. in *You be the Judge* and *Other Worlds*, followed by discussion and/or surveys of opinion and experience amongst friends and family, written work 'What is your opinion about the existence of ghosts?'; *television watching*, facts, figures and opinions discovered through a class questionnaire about viewing habits, preferences, etc., material first presented as graphs, lists, etc., then interpreted and discussed, written work, 'What we discovered about the way we use television'; *space research*; *comparing junior and senior high schools.*

Speeches, articles, statements etc; for description of the preparatory work see *Kinds of Talking – 2.*

Collecting material and forming and exchanging opinions are only the first step in this kind of work. Pupils need a lot of help with finding the most effective way of structuring their written work, particularly with the clear use of paragraphs.

SEQUENCE OF CONTENT

If work in the Department is planned thematically, or organized around key texts, then this should help to impose some order on the material to be studied. One difficulty of thematic structures is that the topics frequently seem to be chosen almost at random – schooldays, the wild west, the sea, the future – without a sense that some are more demanding than others or that the earlier should in some ways be preparing for the later. Indeed, in some schools the project sheets which accompany topics pitch the writing tasks at virtually the same level for 11–12 and 13–14 pupils, rather than assuming that new demands should be made, building on existing progress.

The same criticism might be made of assignments in book-centred classes (write another episode; invent a similar character; say what might have happened after . . .), though if the books have been properly selected then the same tasks will be more demanding if the text itself is more complex. Asking pupils to focus on the importance of fantasy in coping with life, on the interrelation of dream and reality, will be very different according to whether they have been reading Philippa Pearce's *A Dog so Small*, Keith Waterhouse's *Billy Liar* or William Golding's *Pincher Martin*.

Some impression of what sequential planning might involve can be gained by looking at some simple assignment sheets in use in a large comprehensive school. These examples are intended for mixed ability groups in years one, two and three, and the ways in which they are formulated manifest underlying assumptions about young writers' development. Between year one and year three, the suggestions change in a number of ways:

i) from a compulsory topic to increasing choice;

ii) from immediate to more distanced subjects;

iii) from writing in one's own person to writing as another;

iv) from precise specifications, including the suggestion of actual words, to a more open briefing;

v) from full instructions, given in a personal, deliberately stimulating tone to a more impersonal, workmanlike approach.

FIRST YEAR

The incredible shrinking story

Imagine being only a few centimetres high, like a small toy doll. What would the world look like to you? Grass blades would seem like a jungle; stairs like Mount Everest; a baby like a small monster; an adult like a huge giant – and the cat? the furniture? the toys? the models? crossing the road?

Your Uncle Ernest has given you a chemistry set for a birthday present. One day when there's nothing else to do you get it out and mix some of the chemicals together. They make a fizzy, brightly coloured liquid which looks just like a drink. You taste it and immediately you shrink until you're only a few centimetres high. What happens to you?

Write a story in three chapters about you drinking Uncle Ernest's liquid and shrinking

Give it your own title, or use the one at the top of this page. Here are three suggested chapter titles – Chapter One – 'What happened at first when I shrank'. Chapter Two – 'My adventures'. Chapter Three – 'Back to normal size again'.

Your story *could* start like this:

Outside the rain was pouring down. I was bored. There was only the cat to talk to and I had nothing to do. I looked round my room and noticed, under a pile of comics, the chemistry set I'd never even opened....

Don't forget to illustrate your story. It will take several lessons to write it in your books.

SECOND YEAR

Theseus and the Minotaur

Choose to be Theseus, Ariadne or the Minotaur. Tell your story.

1 *If you're Theseus*, make your reader realize your feelings as you arrive in Crete; your feelings about King Minos and his daughter; the sights and smells and sounds of the labyrinth; your first impressions of the Minotaur; the fierceness of the fight; the return and your feelings as you joined Ariadne and the Athenians in the daylight.

2 *If you're Ariadne*, make your reader realize your first impressions of Theseus and the young Athenians; your

continued overleaf

feelings about your father's cruelty; your feelings of danger about helping Theseus; the waiting at the mouth of the labyrinth; your feelings as Theseus returned.

3 *If you're the Minotaur*, make your reader realize how it feels to be shut up at the heart of the labyrinth; whether you are angry to be there, or sad; how you first realized that Theseus was approaching; how the fight became harder than you realized.

THIRD YEAR

Danger

Stories and poems

1 *Imagine being high up* – in a tree, on a mountain ledge, on the Humber Bridge, ready for a parachute jump –
   a) Make a list of words and phrases for what you see, hear, feel and think. *Then*
   b) Write a description, or poem about being high up. Try to write so that your readers will share your feelings.

2 In *Danger*, read the two poems about *being in a tunnel* (pages 90 and 91). Think about them, then *write a story*, real or made up, about a frightening experience underground. Try to make your readers feel what it would be like to be shut up in the dark underground.

3 In *Danger*, look at the *pictures* on pages 8 and 89. Put yourself into one of the pictures and then *write the story* of it.

4 Write a *story about a dare game*, played by a group of people your age. You could make a shy person become brave through the game, or the dare could go frighteningly wrong.

5 People enjoy danger and thrills at *playgrounds and fairs*. Choose one of the machines or rides for your title –

think about the feeling of riding on it, then *write a movement poem* that is as thrilling, and exciting, and frightening as the ride itself.

6 Think back to Bonfire Night, its sights, sounds, smells and feelings. Choose one of these to write about:

a) Write several firework *shape poems* (ask me about these).

b) Write a *longer poem* called *Bonfire Night*. Start with the quiet of early evening; create the noise and excitement of the fire and fireworks; finish with the return to quiet.

c) Write a *story*, real or made up, about one particular 5 November.

[This sheet continues with a number of suggestions for explanatory writing and for group work.]

SEQUENCE OF REMEDIATION

Some language work will need to be based on the diagnosis of difficulties which individuals experience in syntax and structure, spelling and punctuation. Work can then be planned systematically for groups within the class to improve accuracy (See pages 195–204.)

It will be clear that no individual English teacher can plan sequences in isolation; the work needs to be co-operative. Indeed the Schools Council paper goes on to write of the need to establish 'ways of co-ordinating plans with teams of colleagues'. Each of the sequences mentioned here could form the basis for practical investigation within the school: collecting examples of individual children's work over several years as the basis for a longitudinal study or experimenting with using materials or activities in different sequences and analysing the results. Planning is both retrospective and predictive. Its twin aims are to provide the best possible conditions for individual children to develop their abilities and simultaneously to create structures that will reassure children, teachers and others that instruction is systematic.

References

1   Peter Abbs, *Root and Blossom*, London, Heinemann, 1976, p. 21.
2   *Engineering Your Communications*, Engineering Careers Information Service, 1981, p. 9.
3   David Holbrook, 'Student Teacher's Opportunity', *Guardian*, 14 September 1963.
4   Gordon Wells, *Learning Through Interaction*, Cambridge, Cambridge University Press, 1981, p. 273.
5   John D. Gould and Stephen J. Boies, 'Writing, dictating and speaking letters' in James Hartley, *The Psychology of Written Communication*, London, Kogan Page, 1980, p. 96.
6   James Moffett and B. J. Wagner, *Student-centered language arts and reading*, K–13, Boston, Mass., Houghton Mifflin, 1976, p. 149.
7   *Aspects of Secondary Education in England*, London, HMSO, 1979, pp. 81–3.
8   Anne Baker, 'Real Writing, Real Writers', *English in Education*, Autumn 1981, 15, No. 3, p. 4.
9   Donald Graves, 'An examination of the writing processes of seven year old children', *Research in the Teaching of English*, 1975, 9, pp. 227–41.
10 George Sampson, *English for the English*, Cambridge, Cambridge University Press, (1921) 1952 ed., pp. 67–8.
11 ibid., pp. 67–8.
12 C. T. Patrick Diamond 'Teachers' views of writing and their pupils' performance', *English in Education*, Summer 1983, 17, No. 2.
13 Peter Burnhill *et al.*, 'Lined paper, legibility and creativity' in James Hartley, *The Psychology of Written Com-*

munication, London, Kogan Page, 1980, p. 91.

14 Paul Francis, 'An introduction to blob theory', *English in Education*, Summer 1981, 15, No. 2, pp. 17–20.

15 Sara W. Lundsteen *et al.*, *Help for the Teacher of Written Composition, New Directions in Research*, Urbana, Illinois, NCRE and ERIC, 1976, p. 11.

16 Assessment of Performance Unit, *Language Performance in Schools*, Primary Survey Report No. 1, London, HMSO, 1981.

17 E.g. Glenda L. Bissex, *Gnys at Wrk*, Cambridge, Mass, Harvard University Press, 1981; Nancy Martin *et al.*, *Writing and Learning Across the Curriculum 11–16*, London, Ward Lock, 1976.

18 Harold Rosen, 'Progress in composition in the O-level year', *The Use of English*, Summer 1967, 18, No. 4, pp. 229–304.

19 Andrew Wilkinson *et al.*, *Assessing Language Development*, Oxford, Oxford University Press, 1980, p. 222.

20 Kellogg W. Hunt, *Grammatical Structures Written at Three Grade Levels*, Illinois, NCTE, 1965. Also see Frank O'Hare, *Sentence-Combining*, improving student writing without formal grammar instruction, Illinois, NCTE, 1973, pp. 67–76.

21 John Dixon and Leslie Stratta, *Achievements in Writing at 16+*, Birmingham University, 1981.

22 B. J. Pendlebury, *A Grammar School English Course*, Book 1, London, Thomas Nelson, (1959).

23 Assessment of Performance Unit, *Language Performance in Schools*, Secondary Survey Report No. 1, London, HMSO, 1982, pp. 103–4.

24 John Dixon and Leslie Stratta, *Teaching and Assessing Argument*, Birmingham University, 1982.

5

GETTING STARTED

The quest for the 'good idea'

This chapter is concerned with how we get students to begin writing: the related issues of motivating them to want to write and actually launching them on the process. For many teachers this is all-important. The planning of a writing lesson is about good ideas for kicking off; the game itself gets much less attention. Such an attitude was encouraged by the vogue for 'creative writing', as can be seen by looking at the bibliography *Creative Writing in the Classroom*.[1] In that volume, 262 books and articles are listed under the general headings 'Stimuli for writing' and 'General classroom techniques'. Many more are shown as helping to elicit specific written modes: poetry, fiction and drama. Under the heading 'Responding to student work' only twelve items appear. So much stress on initiating work, so little on receiving it, seems unbalanced. It also suggests, though, that it is a good deal easier to think of plausible ways of stimulating writing than to engage with the products of that work. Certainly there is no shortage of suggestions on which teachers can draw, but there is a second danger in concentrating on 'stimuli', starters that their originators say have been found 'effective' or 'successful'. In uprooting them, we leave behind the supporting environment, the context of the work.

The assumption underlying many course books and teachers' guides is that successful ideas for writing can be employed with virtually any group. We are coming to realize, however, that there are considerable differences in how pupils perceive a written assignment and respond to it according to (*i*) their relationship with the person who sets it, (*ii*) the instructions given and (*iii*) the nature and presentation of the initiating stimulus.

i) Groups of students who agreed to teach the 'same' lesson on teaching practice and discuss the results found that their reactions to that lesson and to the writing produced in it varied from 'very successful' to 'unsuccessful'. The chemistry changes according to the personalities involved.

ii) When pupils were handed a picture as the basis for their writing, but given slightly different instructions, their work varied. Those who were told to talk about the picture and then write whatever came into their minds were more likely to produce poems; they wrote easily and spontaneously about their feelings and reactions. Those who were told to discuss the picture and then to write about it saw this as a problem-solving task; they offered interpretations in prose, more directly related to what they saw but more tentative in explaining it. On the surface, the difference between the more 'open' and the more 'closed' forms of instructions may seem slight, but it is clear that students saw them as conveying quite distinct expectations about what they should produce.[2]

iii) A Hull teacher got three groups of pupils to write on the same three topics ('The death of an animal', 'The empty house' and 'Feeling left out') but in different circumstances. Each group wrote on one subject simply from the title given, another after reading a related poem with accompanying questions and on a third after seeing and discussing a related picture. After examining the results, the teacher concluded that the children's choices of treatment were significantly narrowed by either the poem or the picture. There was a greater variety of approaches when they were simply given a title. On the other hand, she felt that the writing was generally more successful when there was an additional stimulus. Writing prompted by poems seemed of greater subtlety and complexity of reaction than writing arising from pictures.[3]

'Good ideas', that is, do not come as neutral packages, to be unwrapped in the classroom, untouched by human hand. They have to be made the teacher's own by being thought through in terms of their place in the group's writing programme, the purposes they may achieve, the detailed organization of the lesson and the most likely ways of motivating individuals. The failure to carry out this imaginative, anticipatory preparation is perhaps the chief reason that inexperienced teachers frame their assignments badly. The preparation and the instructions should answer the unspoken questions:

i) Why are we doing this?
ii) For whom are we supposed to be writing?
iii) What is the teacher particularly looking for?
iv) By what shall we be chiefly assessed?

Enquiries among children and even among university undergraduates found that they were frequently trying to fulfil requirements which they did not clearly comprehend because they had never been explained. One of the dangers of the casual, unpremeditated reminder ('Remember to keep to the past tense' or 'Not too many adjectives this time!') is that it is often construed by children as being the most important concern, and negative instructions ('Don't write in long sentences!') can be particularly inhibiting.

Think of the situation from the point of view of pupils who have just completed a piece of writing. When I talk with them, it seems that they feel more or less happy about what they have done according to how far it fits their notion of what they wanted to say. That criterion will have been affected by what they imagine the *teacher* required of them, the expectations raised by instructions, suggestions or modelling. If these two sets of requirements, these two specifications (what I wanted to achieve; what the teacher required) coincide, then all is well. If much work is returned to the children with comments that suggest a mismatch between the two, then it is important to discover why they have misconstrued the teacher's intentions. Part of the teacher's responsibility is to find ways of ensuring that the model of the work, the specification, which children have in their minds is as similar as possible to the one envisaged by the teacher.

It may now be helpful to consider separately the three basic procedures by which most teachers lead in towards writing: modelling, collecting and sharing experiences and ideas through talk, and providing direct or represented experiences. These are not rigidly separated, of course. Teachers may often combine two or all three in a single lesson, but they perform different functions.

Modelling

Demonstrations of how things are done are as important in learning to write as they are in learning chemistry or cookery. Reading a passage on a given subject, or in a particular mode or style, has traditionally been a way to encourage and to focus children's writing. It is an approach used in countless course-books. So teachers may use Michael Rosen's *The Bakerloo Flea* to stimulate the telling of tall stories, or anthologies like *Meet My Folks* or *Beastly Boys and Ghastly Girls* to lead to word pictures of unusual or awful people, or the *Just-So Stories* to prompt tales that explain *how*. Further up the school, *The Spoon River Anthology* can lead to epitaphs on townsfolk, and Orwell or Huxley to visions of the future.

This is quite unlike the modelling of half a century ago, when the aim was to reproduce a given original as exactly as possible from memory. Here the aim is not sterile imitation, but a personal response that in some particular way is 'after' or 'in the style of' the model. Frequently the writers themselves may be so intent on catching one particular aspect of the original that they are unaware of being influenced in other ways. For example, after encountering paraphrases of 'The Wanderer' and sections of 'Beowulf', one girl wrote a poem called 'The Homecoming'. Here is the central section:

> Frozen, fatigued and longing for land,
> Prostrate men, barely breathing in battered boats
> Drifting over a chill, china blue sea,
> Mild morning breezes fill the sighing sails,
> Sliding the ship softly over the slippery seas.
> No raging, rolling waters to hurry them home,
> No storm striking the weary mast
> Or fiendish fog blinding a wandering wayfarer's eyes,
> Just shining, silvery crests in the morning sun
> And the sea-gull's lugubrious lament.

The surface feature of which Julia was perhaps most aware, the use of alliteration, sometimes seems to distort rather than to assist what she wants to say: 'china blue' and 'slippery' are somehow incongruous images for the 'chill' North Sea; the 'morning sun' hardly chimes with the notion of the men being 'frozen'. It is her less deliberate response to the feel of the original that underlies phrases like 'the sea-gull's lugubrious lament' or the attaching of human epithets to inanimate objects: 'the sighing sails', 'the weary mast'. What is happening in this writing is not primarily a technical exercise, but the writer's own vision modified below the conscious level as well as above it.

There is not much experimental evidence about the effects of literary models on the way in which children write. American sources suggest that systematic, planned use of models for specific purposes is more effective than incidental classroom contacts with literature and that models are more effective when they are discussed and related to experience before writing takes place.[4] In one English study Arthur Walker compared the different ways in which children of 10–11 wrote about animals when they were drawing simply on their own experiences and when they had just heard two short prose or verse passages dealing with those animals.[5] There were, as would be expected, differences between individuals and between schools, but overall there was considerable evidence of what Walker called 'drift': the mirroring of words, phrases or ideas from the passages in the children's work. Most important of all, perhaps, was the evidence that the models were seen as a means of signalling the teacher's expectations. What the literary models seemed to do for these children was essentially to suggest that a creative approach was permissible or desirable, although they were given no more specific instructions than on the previous occasion. Thirty per cent more of the children wrote poems; there was more personal reaction and expression of emotion, more involvement with the identity of the animal. Here is a single example of a pupil's two scripts.

The Cat

1 The cat is a nice pet to have at home if you look after it properly. It feeds on milk, cat food, Birds and mice. The cat will be put outside at night to catch mice then early in the morning it will be let in. Cats can be any shapes and sizes. The cat usually sleeps in a basket or a cardboard box lined inside.

There are many different cats, like a tabby, persian,

siamese, and a tom cat.

Kittens sometimes cats, like to play with wool and string, but they usually get into trouble, for undoing someones knitting.

2 Crawling spitefully,
purring and prowling
the cat slinks out of the door,
through the garden
onto the wall,
his black fur shining in the sunlight.

looking in dustbins,
searching for food,
finding fish bones,
drinking other cats milk
The cat prys round corners
Then pouncing out on a rat,
he eats it up all in one go.

Jane

In the first example, Jane is clearly unaware of what is expected of her. *The* cat is a generalization, not the particular animal of her second piece. The items of information are not arranged in any clear order, and there are a number of conventional fillers ('any shapes and sizes', 'There are many different cats'). The language is rather limp ('a nice pet') because she has been given no view of what the writing is *for*. Who wants to read this? Being asked to write after hearing a poem about a cat transforms her ideas. Jane now feels, by implication, that she knows what is expected of her. In a lively response, a specific cat (he, not it) is described in firm details, with an emphasis on his movements (ten different actions in thirteen lines). There is a clear sense of pattern. The first verse paragraph repeats the structure of two short lines and one long one, and the second works on the repeated initial participles, suggesting continuing actions, before the climactic pouncing on the rat, which gives a firm ending.

We could perhaps make more use than we do of children's work for modelling. Stories from *Imagine* or the annual W. H. Smith literary competition are frequently effective for this purpose.[6] One school that produces its own booklets of proposed activities for particular themes and class readers frequently uses children's work in this way. For example, in a series of units on *The Machine Gunners* come suggestions like these:

> After chapter 13, read the accounts on p.4 that Dawn wrote after she'd read this part of the book. She imagined how Chas must have felt about the fight with Boddser. Think whether you agree with her version. Then – *write Clogger's story of the fight*. Remember to include his thoughts and feelings about Chas and Boddser, and about his own part in the fight.

The reproduced work by Dawn is a lively (illustrated) example of writing from the viewpoint of a particular character, and makes plain the kind of work the teacher is encouraging.

> Write some extracts from the diary of Chas or Audrey. The action of the story began in November 1940 and finished in February 1941. Choose four or five days that they 'wrote up' in their diaries. Remember to include Chas' or Audrey's thoughts and feelings about the events they describe, and drawings or plans. The extracts from the diary Claire wrote (on p. 6) may help to give you some ideas.

If children are to develop the variety of writing abilities at which we aim, then they will need to hear or read many different models of the written language. It is from these encounters with various forms and from their attempts to turn them to their own use that they develop increasing awareness of how one kind of writing varies from another. Of course, different modes of writing, and ones that can be undertaken at different levels of ability, can be developed from a single literary text. Here, for example, is a simple sheet of suggestions used by a mixed-ability class that had been reading a novel by Roald Dahl.

Danny The Champion of the World
Choose at least *one* from each part of this.

Important things in the story
1 Danny and his Dad both love *food*. *First*, make a list of the food which they enjoy. *Second*, read Dad's description of toad-in-the-hole in Chapter 13. *Third*, write about three of your most delicious favourites in a way which will make the reader's mouth water.
2 Dad and Danny love *inventions and plans*. *First*, make a list of all their inventions and plans. *Second*, pick out any which didn't work properly and write a paragraph explaining what went wrong.

People
1 Read again about Danny's teachers in Chapter 12. They are rather unusual! Make up 2 or 3 unusual teachers yourself and write a portrait of each one.
2 Decide which are your 2 favourite people in the story – they could be favourite villains. Give them a title, just as Danny has a title, then write a portrait of each of them.
3 Danny thinks his Dad is 'marvellous', 'exciting' and 'sparky'. If you agree with him, explain all the things which make him such a good father.

Writing your own stories
1 Danny's Dad told marvellous stories. Write a story for children which you could tell them at bedtime. Read about the BFG again before you start.
2 Danny and Dad would certainly have more adventures. Write a story about one of them. Things might go wrong again!

Sharing and collecting

A class of 11-year-olds was talking animatedly. Their teacher, whose arm was in a sling, only interrupted occasionally to put a question, to support with a word of encouragement, to decide who went next. He began with a few general questions: Who had been ill and away from school during the last term? What sort of illnesses? Had anybody been involved in an accident? had to go to hospital? had an operation? A general impression was built up: individuals responded with a few words. Then a confident girl, who had only just returned to school, talked almost uninvited about her attack of flu. There were one or two brief additions ('When *I* had the flu ...'). The teacher said something about the road accident in which he had been involved, and his reactions to treatment. Others wanted to share their experiences. As the interest increased, the teacher divided the class into existing groups and asked them to compare their experiences. He went around the groups listening, occasionally joining in, and giving out paper on which the children could begin to jot down the ideas that would lead to writing experiences so that they could be shared by a wider audience.

Such a lesson fits the recommendation of the Bullock Report that 'personal writing' should largely arise from 'a continually changing context': 'created from the corporate enterprises of the classroom and the individual interests and experiences of the children, cumulatively shared with the teacher and the rest of the group.'[7]

The straightforward principles underlying lessons like this are:

i) The basis is children's own experience, particularly moments that are likely to be vivid and memorable.

ii) Interest is aroused by dealing with occasions that are important to the children.

iii) The events are ones with which definite emotional feelings are likely to be associated.

iv) There is a clear purpose in attempting to realize the experience as effectively as possible in words.

v) Talking about the experience to a real and interested audience is an important first step towards writing about it.

vi) The children learn from one another.

vii) Guided sharing and discussion help to overcome stereotyped, stock responses and to shape the experience.

Especially in the middle years, telling anecdotes in this way is an important way of giving coherence to experience, of coming to understand its significance. There is a fascinating account of one such project and the ensuing written work in the first booklet produced by the Bretton Language Development Unit.[8] The sharing helps to give confidence in one's own way of telling and establishes connections between different people's perceptions of experience. There are key associative phrases: that happened to me, it was like that when ..., I know just how she felt, we once, I'd a friend who ..., there was this boy and he....

Once confidence has been established, some teachers like to work on making recall more precise and graphic as a second stage before writing. When Mary says, 'And in the morning I'd come out in these spots ...' the teacher asks, 'What did they look like?' If the answer is vague, she follows up, 'See it again now. You look in the bedroom mirror and what do you see?' On other occasions the teacher might be asking questions 'What could you hear?' or 'How did you feel?' or 'What did they say about that?'

What occurs when this sharing and shaping of experience does not happen is all too easy to illustrate. When an 11-year-old girl is taken to see her new school and is then expected to write about the experience as a task, rather than talking about it first with others, the teacher receives a formal lifeless response:

The New School
I am going to a new school soon. It's big and tall and got lots of children. The children are large middle-size and small, some are clever and some are thick but I think the old school is best. They have cookery English French and German but maths is the worse subject of all.

The principle of collecting and sharing ideas does not have to be limited to anecdotes about personal experience. Children may be encouraged to contribute ideas that are fictional (my horrible monster, if I had one wish, my dream meal, a mad invention). They may collaborate in building up a class poem on the board, given a simple idea or verbal formula (The only thing that frightens me is ...; Good schools have ...; If I had my way, then...).

One example of such a lesson makes the general principles clear. A teacher has been reading some simple 'list' poems with a second-year class, including 'The Great Lover' by Rupert Brooke and John Clare's 'Pleasant sounds'. He suggests that the pupils might combine to produce a list of these-I-have-hated, gives them a minute to think, and asks for suggestions. The first few are undeveloped and tend to be school or food based (maths homework, the skin on milk, today's stew), but they are accepted and written on the board. More ideas come, some of them rather fuller (having to get up on Monday morning, looking after my young sister) and some of them sparked off by what others have said. Occasionally the teacher prompts, if attention seems to be locked onto one particular topic: 'What sorts of sounds or noises do you dislike most? What kind of weather do you hate?' When the board is full, he asks which phrases seem the most vivid, and then how some of the others can be made more effective. 'The alarm clock' becomes 'the strident clamour of my alarm'. He asks which ones 'go together' and might be combined. 'The skin on milk' and 'school custard' turn into 'the rubbery yellow skin on lumpy custard'. When there are a number of developed ideas, the teacher switches attention to the order in which they should be arranged, and how they should be introduced. The agreed first line is 'Of all the things I hate, the worst are …' a possible sequence is worked out, and the final version is tidied. Apart from the pleasure of accomplishing an acceptable end-product, the work has usefully acted out the composing process. Children have been involved in the essential writing activities: originating ideas and seeing how one leads to another, refining the way in which they are expressed, combining and adapting them, giving them an appropriate order and revising the complete work. A model of composing has been presented not in abstract terms but through practical demonstration, and the fact that the final product on this occasion was not particularly distinguished is relatively unimportant.

It is extremely hard to document precisely the effect of the teacher in encouraging and structuring this kind of sharing of words, images and ideas. Read the following simple piece by a third-year girl:

> I take the lemon from the bowl. It is small and oval and has a tangy smell. When I first cut through the tough yellow skin a spray of citrus juice squirts out. Already my taste buds are reacting. The segments inside are a pale yellow and look juicy and refreshing and they bring a sudden pang of thirst. As I take the first taste I have to close my eyes because of the bitter, sweet and sour taste in my mouth.

This reads like a direct response to an immediate stimulus. The short sentences emphasize the sequence of specific sense impressions. We imagine that we are reading a standard piece of traditional 'creative writing'. Is our impression affected at all when we read this other passage by a third-year boy?

> It's a bright golden yellow it's almost a perfect round shape apart from two bumps at each end. A spray of juice squirted out as I inserted the knife through its skin, my

taste-buds began to twinge and tickle. A lemon-yellow contrast with its skin appeared as I split the lemon in half. My saliva glands began to work overtime and I kept swallowing and licking my lips as the lemon came towards my mouth. I took a bite, bitter juices sprayed around my mouth and the sweet tangy smell made me take more bites.

As we notice the similarities between the two, we begin to doubt the immediacy of the response. Not only do the two writers have a good number of phrases in common (tangy smell, spray of juice, taste buds, bitter, cutting 'through the skin'), they follow the same organizational sequence (appearance of the lemon, cutting it open, salivating, biting and tasting). By gathering on the board words from the pupils' jotted notes and discussing possible arrangements of them, the teacher seems to have influenced the subsequent writing. What is virtually impossible to estimate is how far that influence is beneficial. What would the work have been like without the sharing process? Might it have been improved if these two had not been led to think of taste buds? We notice that there is not too much carbon-copying from over-dominant teacher suggestions. One of these pupils writes in the present and one in the past; one begins with her own action and the other with more detached observation; each has individual perceptions and vocabulary (citrus, segments, saliva).

This variability and unpredictability can be further illustrated by looking at the work of two 13-year-old boys. Their teacher had been working with the group on the experience of being under water, drawing on pictures and reading as well as on their own experience. She had given them some questions to answer, and from these she drew words and phrases which they could share. It is striking how far they make the ideas their own. Christopher's is clearly very much more fluent, but it is Michael – despite his difficulties with language – who has been helped to get inside the experience more vividly.

Swimming under water

From the heat of the sparkling warm Mediterranean climate, to the colder depths of the clear blue sea. The boat became a shimmering shadow. This was the world of sharp golden coral reefs, orange, blue and purple exotic fish, air bubbles sparkling like diamonds in the light above, and small insignificant worm like creatures, wriggling in and out of deep dark cracks in the timeless coral.

It was time to return to the other world far above, the water slowed the ascent down, visions of weird creatures passed by at an unbelievable rate. Everything was distorted. Before long the noises of everyday life returned, the air was crisp and fresh. It was time to leave, the engine on the boat roared and spluttered, the secrets of the depths were left behind for another day, and another time.

Christopher

I dived in the worling riples of the water, with a mout full of air. I could see fish swimming by my eyes. I just tred water and floted dreming of hieven just stud, and then I glide in the water with my bag for spesimins of coral of sea arching. The water felt like a shert of silk droping over me like a bed shet the water summed to hold me up it is grete to glide to the serfis gasping for a breat of a jist despret for one mout full of air.

Michael

Communal composing generally seems best when limited to short pieces built up, like Meccano, from simple units,[9] but some teachers have been successful in using group composition for longer, non-formulaic pieces.[10] A variant of this kind of shared work is to break up a larger piece into component parts, and to set groups of pupils to tackle one part each. Providing that the story-line is clearly decided beforehand, plays can be divided into scenes or larger stories into chapters.[11] Such a project seems to be greeted with enthusiasm, but I have found that it makes considerable organizational demands on the teacher. If continuity between the parts is to be maintained, then it seems necessary to duplicate and circulate work regularly, and to discuss the apparent 'fit'. The other weakness is that, unlike the communal poem described above, such a project is in a number of respects different from the composing process that an individual would carry out.

Group narration, with less teacher involvement, can be undertaken in form as a way of leading in to written stories. Members of each group take it in turn to contribute. At first they may tell one sentence each in rotation: later they may narrate for a minute or simply choose when to hand over to the next teller. The problems of maintaining consistency of tone and of following a narrative line can be discussed in the light of experience and then the group narration can be attempted again. Or a situation may be posed (lost on the moors as darkness falls, finding nobody at home when arriving as invited for a party) and the groups be given five minutes to follow up (*Then* what happens?) and to bring it to a conclusion.

At third or fourth year level, pairs can play a variety of consequences. Give each pupil a picture of a person (or simply the feet or hands) to describe to the partner. Together they have to decide when, where and how these two might meet. Each writes down what 'his/her' character would think of the other, and then in turn they write the ensuing conversation, each providing the words of one character in response to what the other has just said. The conversation has to lead to an agreed conclusion (*Then* what would your characters do? think? feel?).

The sharing may also be intended to lead towards a more unified, communal written outcome. For example, the class or a group may be working on:

i) A village or street, in which each child adopts a particular person (or representative of a particular job or trade) who is to be developed as part of a community.

ii) A welcome to the first visitors from outer space, in which each pupil decides on a particular experience to be shared with the newcomers as 'typical' of Britain.

iii) The Rogues Gallery in which each describes a different criminal or evil-doer.

iv) Virtually any project which aims to build up a collection of connected pieces: a book of interests and hobbies.

One final word of caution. We sometimes assume that if the discussion is lively and interesting then the ensuing writing will be better. This does not always follow. Sometimes the talking itself seems to have satisfied the needs of the group and subsequent writing appears irrelevant. There is no way of predicting the quality of writing from the level of shared talk that has preceded it.

Using direct and represented experiences

The rise and fall of the word 'stimulus' parallels the movement in and out of fashion of the term 'creative writing'. Pictures, music, objects are still commonly used to encourage writing, but teachers are less likely to refer to them as a 'stimulus'. This is in part because of a swing away from the classroom model of one-off, teacher-dominated writing activities detached from the rest of the language programme, and in part because of a rejection of the mechanistic stimulus/ response psychological model that underlay it. The dominant images of the texts provided for teachers and pupils in the 1960s and early 1970s were of two kinds. The one saw the teacher as the provider of raw materials which the children were to process into stories and poems ('Teachers are there to feed new ideas', to 'provide stimuli', 'feeding in' experience). The other saw the teacher as more deliberately manipulating the pupils to trigger off the creative impulse (teachers should 'evoke' or 'heighten' sensations, 'encourage sensuous response', 'release and bring to the surface all the locked-up information', 'transmit ... enthusiasm', 'offer the thrust to action, the spur to creation').[12]

The weakness of such a model was essentially the implied limitation it placed on the roles of the teacher and of the child. Children were commonly seen as passive recipients of stimulus and teachers as providers who then sat back and awaited 'creativity', an original process in which they felt unable to intervene. To reject the model, however, is not to reject the use of direct or represented experience in the classroom. The test is how the experiences are used, what relation they bear to the other work of the group, what kind of thinking and sharing is encouraged, what happens during the drafting process and how the writing is evaluated.

As an example of a more 'programmed' way of using direct experience, here is a lesson taken with 12-year-olds and a possible way of following it up. Each child was given a cellophane-wrapped sweet: a hard green lime-flavoured shell containing a soft chocolate inner. Stage by stage they had to make notes on their impressions of this sweet, as briefed by the teacher. First the appearance and anticipation. Then the unwrapping (what does it sound like?) and the smell. Then the feel and the taste and texture (at least two distinct stages). From their notes they then wrote about their experience. Rather than ending at this point, the teacher might duplicate copies of a number of the children's descriptions (or sections of a larger number) for use in the next period. In groups they can discuss the similarities and differences between their perceptions and particularly the terms and images used to convey the difficult impressions of smell and taste. They can then be asked to write about sweet-eating again (possibly in the form of a poem) employing whatever ideas they wish from the work of others.

There are particular advantages in using non-verbal materials to focus children's attention, since these will not tempt them to adopt the words of other writers, as a literary model might. The range of possible 'starters' is enormous. Here, for example, is one simple check-list provided for education students. It is not intended as a model: the students are told that the most important items are those which they add to or adapt from the list. You may also find considering what is omitted an interesting activity!

(A) DIRECT EXPERIENCE

Isolating single senses

A way of focusing attention and of simplifying choices: identifying sensations, finding words to describe and distinguish them, considering the associations (what does it make you think of? what memories, associations does it have? what feelings does it arouse? what kind of situation can you visualize?). Remember that the vocabulary of taste and smell is much more restricted than the vocabulary of sound and sight.

a) Sight. Because so much used and involved in other experiences (objects, pictures) better to concentrate on a single visual element, e.g. colour (different shades of red, looking through coloured transparencies), shape (different kinds of ball or cube), angle (puzzle pictures), magnifying and diminishing.

b) Sound. Listening for near and distant sounds; miscellaneous recorded sounds (sawing wood, laying table, shovelling coal); distinguishing sounds (engines of car, lawnmower, speedboat, diesel or crowds at different events); sound sequences (school ends for the day, hunt meets, train leaves); sound stories.

c) Touch. Identifying objects by feeling alone; riddles describing objects by tactile qualities; distinguishing feel of objects (fur, china, clay, silk, polythene, rope, washleather); 'if you were blind'.

---

d) Smells or tastes. (Needs careful organization: small bottles for objects to smell, foil packets or wooden spoons for tasting.) Identifying and describing smells of soap, lemon juice, disinfectant, coffee, curry powder, fishpaste; tastes of diced carrot, cheese, cucumber, apple; distinguishing tastes of mixed flour and salt, coconut and sugar; burning joss-sticks or spraying air freshener; describing taste and smell of favourite foods without naming them (more difficult than it sounds).

Combining the senses

Peeling and sharing an orange, opening and sharing a packet of crisps, unwrapping and eating a sweet, blowing bubbles or dandelions, burning paper.

Objects

Chosen to fulfil one of two functions:

i) Directly stimulating: miner's lamp, treasure map, old pistol, early telephone, policeman's truncheon, ornamental casket (what is in it?), bones, a pet animal, rusty key.

ii) Open to a wide range of reactions and treatment: pebbles, pieces of bark, strange ink-blots.

Recorded music

Particularly of two kinds:

i) 'Story' music, like 1812 Overture, Carnival of Animals, Petrushka, Peter and the Wolf, Peter Grimes sea interludes.

ii) 'Open' impressionistic music, e.g. Planets Suite, Pictures at an Exhibition, Symphonie Espagnole, Prelude à l'après midi d'un faune, Penderecki's Threnody, Shostakovich cello concerto.

continued overleaf

Avoid using music which produces stock responses, e.g. a Mozart symphony or a recent 'pop' number.

Experiences outside the classroom

Encouraging the jotting of notes to be written up later:

a) Using the environment: watching workmen on building site, listening to the traffic, looking at shop windows; different types of front door, lighting, pavement surface, manhole covers.

b) Capitalizing on the weather: walking in the fog, feeling the snow, scuffling through autumn leaves.

c) Becoming more conscious of physical activity: running, sliding, swinging, free-wheeling downhill, throwing and catching a ball.

d) Talking with or interviewing people: old folk's memories, shoppers' views of shops and shopkeepers' views, 'what do you like most about ...?' people's views of school.

e) Establishing contrasts: between busy and quiet places, between the same place at different times of day or in different weathers, between the perceptions of different pupils.

(B) REPRESENTED EXPERIENCE

Pictures or slides

a) Scenes of action
   Sequences of work:
   i) describing the picture to someone who has not seen it;
   ii) bringing the picture 'alive' by imagining yourself there and using the other senses;
   iii) putting yourself 'into' the picture as one of the people shown in it;

iv) using it as the basis for a story.

b) Pictures of places: what is it like? what sort of people live here? how would you feel if you lived there? describe a typical day in your life.

c) Pictures of people: describe their appearance; consider what sort of education, home, job, interests they have (compare answers with others); imagine meeting between two people shown (when and where it might happen? how would each react to the other? what happens?); to what sort of people do these hands or feet belong? matching pictures of people with pictures of houses.

d) Pictures of people at work: how would you describe this job? how would you feel about doing it? what does the picture omit that is important?

e) Puzzle pictures: what are these two people thinking and feeling and what would they say to each other? what is this crowd of people looking at and how are they reacting? what is happening here and what can have led up to this? what does this 'open' picture suggest to you?

f) Emotionally loaded pictures: explain your reactions to the subject of this picture and the ideas it arouses in you; what effect does looking at these two pictures together have on you? (slum and mansion, expensive restaurant and starving beggar, rugby scrum and ballet class).

Written material

a) From newspapers and magazines. Intriguing headlines (write the accompanying story); responding to controversial letters or articles; personalizing news stories (if this happened to you); expanding telegram messages into newspaper story; incorporating people or incidents into stories.

continued overleaf

b) From literature. Completing a story from a given opening, or writing to reach a given conclusion; episode 'on the same lines' as example read (big or little like Gulliver, shipwrecked like Crusoe or the boys of *Lord of the Flies*); what really happened in 'Flannan Isle' or other mystery.

c) 'Translation' or re-creation

    i) Of viewpoint: giving the old man's view of the boys in *Grandad with Snails*; seeing the trial in *To Kill a Mocking Bird* from viewpoint of different participants; the messenger reports to the Duke about 'My Last Duchess'.

   ii) Of period: modern Canterbury pilgrims; Jane Eyre goes to a comprehensive or Billy Caspar goes to Dr Arnold's Rugby; a present-day Long John Silver or Mr Squeers.

  iii) Of form: stories or episodes from novels become comic strips, radio plays, scripts from TV or film; Carrie writes her diary or a letter; a formal report on Lennie's death in *Of Mice and Men*; a scene from a play is turned into a story.

  iv) Of effect: turn the pleasant scene into a sad or dreary one; present an unattractive character in a good light; make the serious incident into a comic one; turn the climax into anti-climax.

Talk

a) Shared experiences or anecdotes: about pets or other animals; occasions when you got into trouble; friends and enemies; my most frightening, amusing, embarrassing experience; telling strange dreams or tall stories.

b) Improvisation and role-playing: family argument about where to go for holiday; trouble with the neighbours; deciding who should do the jobs.

c) Decision making or problem-solving: how would you get out of this situation? what six portable things would you take if you were going to be shipwrecked on a desert island? what items could be buried in a capsule to give future men a vivid impression of life in the late 20th century?

Media

a) Film or television excerpts. Consider series like *Picture Box* and *Writers' Workshop*, *The English Programme*, BFI Film Study extracts.
b) Schools radio programmes. Try series like *Speak*, *Listening, Talking and Writing, Books, Plays, Poems*.
Study the teacher's notes and pupils' booklets (where provided) and preview the material to decide precisely how much is going to be useful.

The first words

One of the dangers of stimulus-hunting was that it suggested that the right 'trigger' would not only provide material for writing but also provide incentive, make the children eager to write. The young teacher was encouraged to focus on the chosen experience rather than on the way in which that experience was to be embodied in writing by different individuals. Children's difficulties in those initial moments, getting the first words on to paper, are echoed by older students.[13]

The teacher, too, has considerable organizational difficulties at that key moment of switching from the active, sharing, often exciting work in talk and actual experience to the lonely, individual, private act of writing. We have all had these difficulties: the disappointed cries of 'It's boring!' 'Do we *have* to?' 'I can't think of anything!' 'What are we supposed to do?' Individuals suddenly want ink, a pen, a new book, paper, advice, permission to leave the room. Meanwhile the disaffected progressively increase noise and misbehaviour, in the hope that they will convert the lesson into a free period. The children who actually want to write begin to complain, 'Oh tell 'im, miss'. The neutral watch the struggle and await the outcome.

There is no possibility of giving one all-purpose remedy to fit every classroom. Experienced teachers often confess that their apparent success in coping is largely a confidence trick, built up over the years. Observation and discussion suggest that their practice is marked by –

- *i*) an appearance of assurance which rejects negative criticisms;
- *i*) clarity of instructions, which are possibly reinforced on the blackboard;
- *iii*) brevity of transition from other activities to writing, helped by having all necessary materials ready;
- *iv*) attention to the whole class: a refusal to deal with individual problems until the group as a whole has settled.

With some teachers it is almost a hypnotic process; you feel the children 'going under' as they begin to compose.

There are some practices that make starting very much more difficult, and contrasting ones that make it easier. We are not considering here those children who have real writing difficulties, but the class as a whole. Beginning is made more difficult if we –

- *i*) insist that all work is fully planned before writing begins;
- *ii*) expect the assignment to be neatly presented and free from crossings-out or alterations;
- *iii*) demand a long period of silent writing;
- *iv*) set topics which have not been adequately prepared by shared experiences or talk;
- *v*) give only a vague impression of what is wanted or the criteria by which it will be assessed.

If we assume that the real problem lies in getting the words flowing, then the following principles and practices may be helpful:

i) Try to overthrow the model of writing that suggests that the whole piece should be planned and clear in the head before the pen touches the paper. Holding back from writing simply makes starting more and more difficult. Encourage the idea that meaning evolves in the act of writing. Assure the children that first drafts are not going to be examined as though they were finished products. (See the last section of Chapter 6.)

ii) Use some of the group collective writing ideas mentioned on pages 116–18 as a way into individual work.

iii) Use the technique developed from the work of James Moffett, starting from a memory chain and going on to develop one item from that chain. This is how the workshop process is described by the New York City Writing Project:

(A) Spontaneous flow of memories

Look around the room or out the window at different things until you see something that reminds you of something from your past (a place, a person, an event). Write the object on which you focused, draw an arrow, and write the memory which it triggered. Now, what other memory does this person, place or event remind you of? Continue writing your memories for 15 minutes, letting the previous one remind you of another one. Do this quickly, in whatever form is comfortable for you (use arrows to show the connections, if you like). Avoid going into detail about one particular memory. When you are finished, you should have a series of memories which may or may not be related to each other.

Classroom Tips

1 When doing this with your students, model the associ-

ation process at the board before the class attempts it.

2 Have student volunteers read their memory chains to the class. The class will be curious and interested to hear them.

3 Focus the discussion on the process of doing this part of the assignment: *how* students wrote memories, types of memories, sequence of memories (if any), *feeling* or *idea* that connects the memories in some way.

(B) Free writing on one memory

Choose one memory from your 'chain' and underline it. Rewrite it at the top of a new page. Then write, quickly, all the details you can remember about this memory – sense impressions as well as observations. Avoid stopping to worry about errors. Write for about 15 minutes.[14]

iv) Encourage jotting, rough notes, spontaneous ideas. Suggest that pupils do *not* struggle to find a first sentence, but begin getting down the ideas that they particularly want to include, and then later think about how to lead up to these. Perhaps give a time limit (How many ideas can you get down on paper in two minutes?) Sometimes it helps to suggest that a pair of students try to think of several different possible openings, from which one can later be chosen.

v) Consider dividing the time. Instead of giving forty minutes to produce a piece (in which case, some pupils will probably finish after twenty) suggest that they write for 15 minutes, then look back over what they have produced, discuss it, and then write it again in the last 20 minutes. Don't give the impression that they are making a 'fair copy'. It *may* be better for them to put away the first version before starting on the second.

vi) Try to help the transition from composing in talk to writing. Persuade children to begin with the words they have just said to their partner, to talk to themselves in the head as they write, to imagine an actual person to whom they are telling this on paper. In some cases, offer all-purpose opening words which can be copied and then followed, e.g.

What happened was this ...

If you want to know my opinion, I think ...

What I liked most was ...

References

1 Robert Day and C. G. Weaver, *Creative Writing in the Classroom*, Urbana, Illinois, NCTE and ERIC, 1978.

2 *Writing Across the Curriculum 11–13*, Associated schools pack 'Taking up a task'.

3 A small-scale investigation carried out as part of her MEd course work by Judith Atkinson.

4 Sara W. Lundsteen *et al.*, *Help for the Teacher of Written Composition, New Directions in Research*, Urbana, Illinois, NCRE and ERIC, 1976.

5 Arthur Walker, 'The effect of literary models on the writing of children (ages 10–11)', BPhil dissertation, Hull University, 1976.

6 R. Protherough and J. Smith, *Imagine*, London, Harrap, 1974; *Children as Writers*, annually, London, Heinemann. Some source books also print pupils' work alongside the writing of major authors (e.g. Christopher Copeman and Graham Barrett, *Feelings into Words*, books 1–3, London, Ward Lock, 1976).

7 *A Language for Life*, Report of the Bullock Committee, London, HMSO, 1975, 11.5.

8 *Stories from Personal Experience 9–11*, Bretton Hall, 1981.

9 There are some useful practical suggestions in Sandy Brownjohn, *Does it Have to Rhyme?*, London, Hodder & Stoughton, 1980.

10 See, for example, M. S. Morris, 'An experiment in group writing', *Use of English*, Summer 1964, 15, No. 4, p. 259.

11   Another variant is described in P. N. Davies, 'A group epistolary novel', *Use of English*, Autumn 1977, 29, No. 1, p. 20.

12   These ideas are considered at greater length in my article 'When in doubt, write a poem', in *English in Education*, Spring 1978, 12, No. 1, p. 9.

13   E.g. 65 per cent of students helped by the Writing Tutorial Service at Ottawa University had difficulties with the initial and pre-writing stages of their work (Aviva Freedman, 'During Not After', *English in Education*, Spring 1980, 14, No. 1, p. 2).

14   Workshop prepared by Marcie Wolfe, New York City Writing Project, 1980.

6

THE COMPOSING PROCESS

Learning about the process

Two related questions have to be asked: How can teachers better understand the process of composing in writing? How far should they try to make their pupils more consciously aware of that process? Clearly the answers given to the second will depend on those made to the first. The difficulty is that whereas initiating writing has been endlessly discussed – as was suggested in Chapter 5 – the subsequent writing behaviour has been little examined. Three sources of insight are worth consideration: our own experiences, those of children and those of professional authors. From these we may be able to help pupils to relate the group teaching–learning process in class to the individual act of writing.

THE TEACHER AS WRITER

It is easiest to begin by thinking about our own writing: the composing activity which we know best. As soon as we begin to reflect consciously about what happens when we ourselves have something to write, however, we realize the limits of our understanding. Before we make the first marks with our pens, we shall have gone through a complex process, much of which is at a subconscious level, formulating more or less what the experiences are which are demanding expression, why and for whom we are writing, and what the focus and the form of the writing will be. Often our ideas will change as we actually write. How we get our ideas, how we make our choices, how we select our opening words – these are matters that we do not fully understand. We know from experience that these things happen and that particular circumstances seem to make the process easier or harder, but that is about all.

Teachers who themselves regularly write generally seem more aware of what their children are having to do than those who do not. Even if all English teachers do not expect to be authors of poems and stories, in the way that art teachers seem to paint and sculpt, they can gain enormously from performing the kind of imaginative task they regularly assign to their students.[1] Those who have taken part in workshops with me, here and abroad, have frequently reported that for years they have not had the experience of writing a poem or story, or being asked to respond to a particular starting-point, or having to write to order within a time limit. They generally go on to say that their first reaction to such a demand is one of fear or resentment but that this is followed by interest, a sense of achievement and – significantly – greater understanding of what the process involves. Actually writing at the same time as students on the same assignment and later sharing the results is an activity which is enlightening (and sometimes humiliating). From the pupils' point of view, they gain confidence from seeing that their teachers also have difficulties, need to revise, and have to learn ways of tackling problems.

Professional writers who have worked in schools either on

brief visits or in a more extended way report children's insistent interest in the practical details. They want to know 'how one writes – exactly what takes place on an ordinary working day ... all kinds of practicalities and methods' says Ronald Blythe.[2] They may feel that their teachers lack this kind of experience, and it would clearly be beneficial if we could let them in on our own understanding of what trying to write involves.

Perhaps the most important benefit of being a teacher-writer is that it makes you more diffident about your expectations: learning and teaching go together. Some of the effects of being a professional author on a classroom teacher have been described by Richard Potts:

> When asking children to write from within themselves I try to remember my own difficulties.... Certainly I would not care to function creatively in an enclosed classroom with 30 other people carrying out the same assignment as myself ... Perhaps we are not always aware of what we are asking of children. I do know that if success is to be achieved with anything more than a minority of a class, then a flexible approach is essential.... The class write in silence, and I write with them on the same topic.[3]

WHAT CHILDREN SAY

Although children's retrospective accounts of their own writing need to be treated with care, they are essential to our developing awareness of composing in school. For example, when representative groups of pupils of different abilities were asked how they got their ideas for writing and what sources they drew on in preparing to write, a difference seemed to emerge between the responses of pupils of 11–13 and those who were older. Children in the first two years of secondary school were much more likely to describe writing as manipulating material, frequently fed to them by the teacher, in a set way. Their sources were seen in straightforward terms: characters, incidents, scenes were freely available to be 'lifted' from television and books (overwhelmingly the two most frequently mentioned sources of ideas). They said things like 'I use bits from books'; 'if I have read a good story I tend to write a story like it'; books provide 'things which will fit into my stories'; 'if I have seen something interesting on television I include it in a story'. In the third year, pupils were much more likely to dismiss such a mode of operation. Remarks like 'I do not copy anything' or 'I got my ideas from myself' suggest that they feel they have grown out of the stage of direct borrowing. They are more likely to point to circumstances in which the imagination can flourish. A boy says, 'I get a lot of ideas when I go fishing, because I can sit and think about things in peace ... also when you are being quiet you notice things more.' A girl says, 'When I go out cycling this helps me and gives me ideas; I take in the new surroundings and what it feels like with the wind pushing hard against me.'

Third-year pupils still see secondary experience as important, of course, but they are more likely to stress how this extends their first-hand knowledge. For example, a girl who wanted to describe a fight said that 'it would have been difficult to write about it had I not seen numerous ones on tele as I have never seen a proper fight, where they were fighting to kill'. A boy felt that television pictures gave him 'a better idea of how things look after accidents or explosions and how everything goes on after these events'. A girl explained that 'I once described an old man's loneliness and there had been a documentary on old tramps and doss-houses the night before.'

Students of 13 or 14 are also more likely to draw unprompted on their own experiences, though the process may not always be as simple as one girl suggests: 'Your own actual experiences are the easiest things to write about, as you were there, so therefore know exactly what to write about and how to write it.' Some of the ways in which pupils are conscious of incorporating actuality can be briefly illustrated:

> We wrote a piece on leaving home, and I put an argument into my work that I had had with mum, but of course I make it sound worse!

> In my first story 'First Encounter'... I wrote about arriving in an empty town... This happened to me in Cornwall when my family and I went to a town only to find it deserted, with everyone at a fair.

> My grandma explained about what happened around Hull during the Second World War and this gave me a good outline when I wrote a piece on an air raid.

In more general terms they mention the way in which 'People I see around me give me ideas for characters', or 'I watch people going about their life and they usually give me ideas', or 'Actual things that have happened and feelings, like if your girl-friend finishes with you'.

Third-year students also show much more awareness of imaginative writing as involving the synthesizing of information drawn consciously or subconsciously from different sources. One boy wrote a story in which 'finding a bomb on a disused railway embankment occurred'. Elements in the original idea were drawn from novels and non-fiction, film and television. They were given shape and precision, though, by setting the event in a place known to him near the school: 'A railway used to run through Willerby, and I imagined the bomb to be found on one part of the embankment.' Several of these pupils talk of words, ideas, impressions 'sticking' unbidden in their minds and surfacing when needed. 'I once read a story where a ghostly force took over a house and made things happen. That has stuck in my mind and when I mixed it with a programme I saw on TV I got a different story altogether.' Her notion of 'mixing' two elements to produce a new compound comes across as rather mechanical but others see the process as initially subconscious and almost insidious ('I sometimes find the plots of books creeping into my own ...'). A number are half-aware of complexity which is too difficult to put into words: the way in which a dream, or 'a quick glimpse of something sparks off an idea', the notion that in the act of writing impressions and words 'from many different places are put together'.

It seems that in years one and two teachers are perhaps right to emphasize the provision of appropriate models, experiences and materials, without worrying too much about the way in which last night's play gets dragged into the writing. In years three and four, however, we can build on an increasing awareness of the creative process. Because of children's developing realization of the different methods and circumstances which 'work' best for them, topics for the whole class may be less useful, and attention may shift increasingly to ways of using source material. This impression is reinforced by children's evaluation of the writing programmes they have followed.

At the end of the school year, four classes, two in the second year and two in the third of a large comprehensive school, were asked to suggest which piece of writing completed in English during the year they had most enjoyed doing and to try to indicate the reasons for their preference. The impressions which emerged, and which might prompt comparisons in other schools, were:

i) The range of choice. At least eight different pieces of writing were mentioned in each class: ten or eleven in some. No single topic was mentioned by as many as half the children in a class. This seems to emphasize the importance of variety in the writing programme: different individuals responded to different subjects, there were no universal favourites.

ii) The range of modes. Although stories were most mentioned, some children's favourite pieces were plays and poems, essays, reviews and TV scripts. A number of boys said specifically that they preferred to write 'factual', 'non-fiction' pieces.

iii) The apparent preference for long pieces of work. In the second year the Desert Island project was the most frequently mentioned piece of writing, and in the third year the 'novels' in several chapters. This liking for extended work may be because of the sense of achievement or because it seemed less teacher-controlled than shorter pieces.

Second-year pupils found it hard to explain why they had chosen one piece of writing: they simply 'enjoyed writing about that', it was 'fun', 'interesting' or 'exciting'. A number of them referred specifically to what the teacher had provided to help them: the work was enjoyable because they had an 'information booklet', or pictures, or guidelines to help in structuring the work. They also mentioned, as did students a year older, the importance of work in which they could express their own 'imagination', their feelings and ideas. The third-year pupils concentrated much more on the circumstances in which the writing was done. The most frequently mentioned ideas were freedom of choice, the ability to work in groups or to discuss a project, the opportunity of writing at length and the chance to work at home. A few extracts give the flavour:

I enjoyed writing my 'novel' most as I could get on with it at my own speed and could write it when and where I liked which I find is more enjoyable to do than having to sit down in a classroom at a set time and get on with the work.

I enjoyed writing my 'novel' the most this year, probably because I had picked what I had wanted to write and could do anything I wanted with my characters. I could express my feelings on paper without actually involving myself in person. This meant that after I had finished writing, I felt happy and at peace having given away some of my stronger feelings to my story. I also enjoyed being able to write for a long time or for only a short time and not really having to work to a deadline, so if I became stuck I could leave it until I knew what and how I was going to carry on writing.

I prefer to write my poems and short stories in complete quiet or at home. I also prefer to write about myself or things around me which are familiar to me ... I like my work better when it comes from within me otherwise when I am trying to write a piece on some situation I am not familiar with it seems fake or silly.

THE ACCOUNTS OF AUTHORS

If anybody knows what it is like to write, then it should be an established author. Unfortunately, authors are not always good at self-analysis: their descriptions are inevitably highly personal, their retrospective accounts cannot necessarily be trusted, and their chief concerns tend to be with the circumstances – the conditions, their blocks, the criticisms, their agents and publishers – rather than with the process of writing. We have a whole series of idiosyncratic accounts of the circumstances which particular writers found helpful – or even essential – to the creative process: Coleridge waking from an opium dream with a poem in his mind, Balzac drinking vast quantities of black coffee, Schiller plunging his feet in icy water and inhaling the smell of rotten apples, Zola hiding from the daylight, Housman walking for hours and trying to keep his mind inactive as he gazed at the scenery. Some writers have found it essential to write with a particular pen or ink or paper, or to sit at a particular place, or even to wear certain clothes. Such facts have their fascination, but are not of much direct help to the teacher.

The clear variations in authors' practices may persuade us that it is unwise to insist that all our children compose in one uniform way. Professional writers compose at very different rates, often varying from one book to another. Some always make detailed outlines before they begin to write, others never do. Some draft a whole section and then revise it, others combine drafting and revising throughout. We cannot base school practice on such a shifting foundation. On the other hand, the different ways in which authors get and develop their ideas may be used to suggest to children how writers work.

The work of writers for children may be particularly helpful, especially for pupils who have read their books. One volume of interviews with such writers[4] suggests a fruitful tension between the unconscious and the conscious activities of the mind. The original impetus, the idea for the book, may come from anywhere: a chance suggestion, an unexpected present, something seen or heard by chance, a memory, a page in another book. It may have been deliberately sought or it may come out of the blue, but it nearly always seems somehow 'given'. The idea may be consciously worked on and developed over a long period, or it may be immediately followed, with no idea where it will lead. Barbara Willard says:

> The way an idea for a book turns up in your mind is usually quite different from the way you finally write the story. You can wake up in the morning with an empty mind, and by the time you go to bed that night, you have a whole book worked out, or you can sit down and write Chapter One, and really and truly you do not know what's going to happen after the end of Chapter One at all. You can't lay down any rules about this.[5]

Nearly all the children's authors represented in those interviews say that they have a situation, theme or plot clearly in mind before they write, but also that – however detailed the initial plan – it always changes. Joan Aiken says that her plots 'gradually accrue'. 'What I try to do is to start off with some crisis or problem situation ... I do, in fact, work out the plot entirely before I start to write, but then it often changes as I go along'.[6]

The combination of the known and the unknown, the planned and the spontaneous, seems universal. The writer is neither wholly the craftsman, knocking up the box according to planned specifications and drawings, nor the gardener, tending the organic processes of the plant until it blooms.

The conscious preparations will usually involve bringing together from direct and secondary experience events, scenes, people, ideas that the author is anxious to write about. Barbara Willard has described how she wanted to deal with a vast holly plantation near where she lived, and with the iron industry that had earlier existed where she now lived, and with the theatre world in which she had been brought up, and 'so I put all these ideas together, and they turned into the story *The Grove of Green Holly*'.[7]

The sense of preparedness frequently comes from the grounding in personal experience. Kathleen Peyton has said that, with one possible exception, 'every book I've written so far ... is definitely written through things I've done'.[8]

The strongest sense of being rooted in a particular locality and tradition comes across in the books of Alan Garner, the fantasies and *The Stone Book* quartet. Garner himself has said that when he decided to be a writer,

> I turned to the thing which I knew best, which is what every writer does. In my case, it was Alderley Edge. The books are fantasies, but they take place in a real setting, here and now. I think this is very important. It is for me, anyway – to write fantasy in a place where the reader can go and see and touch and experience for himself.[9]

Some themes demand more deliberate and lengthy preparation, particularly for writers of historical fiction. Rosemary Sutcliff says that for her 'half the fun of writing a book is the research entailed',[10] and Lucy Boston and Barbara

Willard tell similarly of the need to 'learn' before writing.

However 'fixed' in actuality or research the work may be, however, it still has to leave room to grow in the course of writing. Both Joan Aiken and Nina Bawden talk of reading their stories to their own children chapter by chapter, and changing direction in the light of their comments. The notion of unpredictable growth or development during the process of writing has been vividly described by Penelope Farmer. She says that she always plans a book in detail, and prepares an 'outline' or 'synopsis', but that this is really there to provide what she calls a 'kicking-off point'.

> Very often you find the whole plot changes. Things happen in the plot which could never have happened before you've actually written a part of it. In some instances the plot naturally springs from what you've written, where it probably wouldn't have occurred to you before. It comes spontaneously, all at once. You get an idea, and it is just a little silly thing, and it might sound very insignificant and unimportant. It grows gradually bit by bit. You walk down the street and you see something that gives you another idea. You add it in, or you may not. You may find you want to add it in but it doesn't quite fit, and you fiddle around with it. Finally, somehow, it slides into place in the plot, or it doesn't and you chuck it out. You must always allow for this; you must allow for things developing. Sometimes the things that develop are much better than the original, sort of mechanical, setting out of the plot.[11]

The notion of gaps, of indeterminate areas into which new ideas can come almost unsought, sometimes changing the whole structure, is a common one. Once the mind has been focused on the writing it somehow becomes sensitive to these illuminations. Kathleen Peyton says that she often has these moments while sitting on a train; her husband while he is in the bath; Michael Bond on bus journeys; Lucy Boston while sitting alone by the fire in the evening.[12]

DIRECT OBSERVATIONS OF CHILDREN

When we watch a class of children writing, we are struck by the variety of behaviour we see. Some pupils begin work immediately, others need to talk or think for a long time. Some will write almost without stopping, whereas others break off frequently, pause, look back over what they have written, think and start again. Some crouch over with their heads nearly on the paper, some keep changing position, some lean back at a distance from their work. Some will be deeply immersed, cut off from the world, but others will be constantly looking around, seeking the eye of teacher or friend. We observe these variations, but we have only the sketchiest idea of what is going on in those different heads as their hands obediently transcribe words on paper.

Because empirical studies have almost always focused on the written product rather than on the writer's behaviour while writing, we are short of information about how children actually write. There are no real answers to questions like these:

  i) Do children write differently at home from the way they do in school?
 ii) How much of their 'writing' time do children spend on thinking, planning, talking, revising and other activities?
iii) Do the proportions of time spent on these different activities vary much according to the task set?
 iv) Are there significant differences in writing behaviour according to the arrangement of the classroom?
  v) Is there any correlation between speed in writing and quality of the final product?
 vi) Under what conditions do children actually start to write and decide to finish writing?

Attempts to analyse the composing process have been initiated in the USA by Janet Emig, who got older students to compose aloud while writing, and by Graves and others in the

1970s, through detailed observation and interviews.[13] In this country Alex McLeod and John Richmond have done particularly interesting work, especially by using TV cameras to record simultaneously on videotape the writing being done by pupils and their faces while writing.[14] Beyond the emerging data and the apparent conclusions – some of which will be mentioned briefly in the next section – there is an important implication for classroom teachers.

If we feel that certain kinds of observation about the writing procedures of our children would be helpful, then there is no need to wait for the researchers. The classroom itself is the research laboratory, and any English department can carry out its own investigation.[15] Students in training, working individually with a teacher or as a group, can help with such work at the same time as they learn how to observe by being given a particular focus. By watching selected children during a twenty minute spell of writing, they can record such information as the length of time these children actually spend writing and the length of the 'bursts' of writing, or the apparent reasons for which they break off (to talk, to look around, to read a book, to revise, to think). The observers may also be able to note the points in the writing at which stops recur, and the relationship between the amount of time spent writing and the number of words written. Are there differences in writing behaviour between boys and girls, between different maturity levels, or between different kinds of writer (like the *reactive* and *reflective* distinguished by Graves)? Do different topics or kinds of writing activity seem to be associated with different behaviours?

Implications for classroom practice

If we combine our own experiences of writing, our observations in the classroom, and the evidence of what children and authors say, then certain practices seem to follow as likely to be helpful.

a) There needs to be a great deal of writing, on a wide range of subjects and in a variety of modes, in a climate which will encourage children to draw freely on their own experience and to be prepared to experiment in language.

b) Writing is a process of discovery as well as a communication of the already known. For this reason, assignments need to balance the planned and the spontaneous, elements of freedom and choice with the controlled and the restricted. Dissatisfaction with the set teacher-directed lesson, involving writing to be done on the spot, seems to increase with age.

c) Because children differ in their responses, tastes, speeds and methods of writing, they should not be led to think that all must plan, write and revise in just the same way. It may be possible to adapt classroom procedure and organization to fit different needs (e.g. allowing some to work in groups or pairs and others to work quietly and individually in another part of the room).

d) Some assignments should either be long ones spread over a period of weeks or ones where there is a delay between initiation and collection of the work, so that there is room for 'growth', for creative ideas to come unsought, or for rehandling after reflection.

e) As well as providing experiences and models which will spark-off initial ideas, teachers may need to concentrate on ways of building up and combining materials from different sources, 'realizing' ideas in specific images or making notes 'from life' as the basis for writing.

f) Because of the shift in attitude that seems to come for many pupils between the second and third years, there may need to be more deliberate emphasis on the 'craft' of writing from age 13 onwards. Some possible activities are described on pages 150–5.

What happens during writing?

Much of what passes for guidance about the writing process is folk mythology: beliefs are held in the teeth of conflicting opinions and evidence. Compare, for example, these confident assertions:

 i) It's very simple. If children really want to write, they just write.
 ii) The basic stages of composition are the same for any form of writing. First the writer chooses the subject, then he assembles and organizes his materials to provide an outline, and finally he drafts and revises his composition.
 iii) Creativity is the illumination of sudden intuitions about experience which the writer wishes to share by providing verbal equivalents for the original stimuli which caused the experience.
 iv) This model of composition involves planning, generating knowledge, translating into speech and editing.

The picture is very different according to whether you consult a no-nonsense teacher, a traditional composition textbook, a creative writer or a communications theorist.

At the extremes, the two diametrically opposed views of written composition are the one which sees the writer as awaiting the divine spark and then writing as an unplanned, almost automatic process and the other which sees writing as a matter of following a sequence of invariable steps, like a cookery recipe. Neither holds good for more than some writers on some occasions dealing with certain subjects. Both are exposed by the sorts of insight briefly summarized on pages 143–4. When we look at our own writing, or our pupils', we are conscious chiefly of a variety of things happening all at once. It is true of me as I write these words. I have a plan on paper that is being changed as I go. In writing the last page a new idea has come that I am afraid of forgetting. I have remembered that something similar was in a book recently read and must check it. It will be necessary to alter one piece in the last chapter in the light of what I have just written. On re-reading this paragraph I am aware that there's too much repetition, and that I must revise. And so on. It has been demonstrated that during composition people do not follow any one set sequence of activities but shuffle to-and-fro between initiating ideas, relating items, writing, revising and proof-reading.[16]

In other words, rather than thinking about static *stages* in the composing process it seems more helpful to think of *processes* that are constantly being combined and re-combined dynamically. The terms applied to stages like preparation, illumination, resolution, are real enough. We *do* plan, gather materials, search our memories, imagine our audience, make decisions about form, tone or structure, seek for the right word or image, check back over what is written, ponder about outcomes, revise and correct. However, we are rarely, if ever, doing these things one at a time. The central difficulty of writing is that it demands that we should carry out a number of these operations simultaneously. There are limits to the number of concerns which the brain can be conscious of at any one time, but the writer – and particularly the *young* writer – is frequently dealing with more considerations or constraints than can be easily accommodated. It is this above all that accounts for so much of the weakness of school writing. To caricature it for simplicity, imagine the different conscious and subconscious concerns now in the mind of that boy writing and pausing and writing again in his desk by the window. What exactly does the teacher really want? Can I work in that bit from last night's television? How much more do I need to write? How do you spell accumulate? Shall I use another word? Will she mind if I use swear words? Have I written as much as Peter? Were we meant to put in conversation? How can I end this? Will she give me a better grade this time? Should I put in a bit more description? Why is my handwriting so untidy? Should that be a fullstop or a comma?

Writing involves different processes at different levels of difficulty and complexity. In mature writers, many of these have become virtually automatic. We do not normally need to occupy our minds with thinking about spelling or punctuating correctly, about paragraphing or laying out a letter, or about turning inner speech into legible written form. The problem for children can be simply thought of as one of *overload*. They are engaged in so many processes simultaneously, so much of their attention is demanded by low-level skills, that the more complex considerations (of structure and style, say) are simply driven out of mind. This helps to explain, for example, why most children write personal anecdotes earlier and much more fluently than they do fictional ones. For the personal story, the mind re-runs the film of memory, and attention can be concentrated on finding verbal equivalents for the events. For the invented story, the mind has the additional tasks of creating incidents and characters, of relating these in terms of motivation and causality, and giving the whole a conventional structure. It is no wonder that younger children try to make the task possible by borrowing the narrative from film or television.

The notion of overload helps to explain why some pupils' work occasionally disappoints us. For example, it is when young children are most excited and carried away by a topic that they often make most mistakes. They have been so dominated by the subject, their pens have been moving so fast, that little of their attention has been left for punctuation and structure. In a different way, trying to handle a new form systematically on paper can swallow up concern for interest or readability. A 14-year-old, asked to write on 'Shall homework be abolished?' is so conscious of needing to organize the material appropriately that the writing is uncharacteristically dull and stilted:

There are two sides to this argument both which have many good points for and against the abolishment of homework.

On one hand homework should be abolished because if someone's parents specialise in a subject such as French that someone may not work as hard in French as he does in other subjects and most likely will get help with his French homework also masters may get the wrong impression of a boys homework as he could easily of collaborated with some other members of his form.

and so on, for nearly three pages.

In these terms, development in writing can be thought of as the ability to handle increasing numbers of processes simultaneously, or as the ability to make some of them automatic and to make deliberate choices between others. Learning can be defined as the acquisition of sufficient mastery of a particular process to enable the writer's attention to be diverted elsewhere. Thus children who operate exclusively in Britton's 'expressive' mode tend to give most of their attention simply to getting the words down on paper. They write what they think just as they think it, as they would in speech. They are normally pleased with their work when the subject is congenial; the topic determines the degree of success. As the act of composing in writing becomes easier, more attention can be given to correctness. Frequently the fact of thinking more about spelling, punctuation and sentence construction can mean that the quality of the writing, apart from the mechanics, can degenerate for a while. Again, as competence in these different skills increases, so it becomes possible for the writer to consider rather more the fact that work is to be read. Increasingly pieces can be differentiated according to the audience and the purpose which the writing is supposed to achieve. In turn, as this becomes more instinctive, so there is the possibility of viewing one's work critically, of developing a personal style, of handling more complex literary forms.

This kind of progress is not to be seen as an invariable sequence, a neat hierarchy in which one higher ability succeeds another lower one. We are all aware that in certain situations and on particular topics children can produce work that is well ahead of their usual performance. Pupils whose writing is still egocentric can sometimes produce strikingly empathetic work; those who are normally incoherent can create well-structured narratives when the event is important to them. We can explain these atypical results, though, not simply in vague terms of motivation but by suggesting that the particular process involved has temporarily become dominant, to the exclusion of others, which might otherwise be seen as constraints. One of the most important and helpful roles of the teacher, then, is to reduce the number of competing constraints for pupils.

We can help to avoid overload in a number of ways. First, we can encourage children to separate out the processes of composing and transcribing, helping them first to get their ideas down rapidly and then to give more thought to such qualities as neatness, spelling and punctuation. Second, we can indicate which of the competing constraints are to be seen as most important for the particular piece of writing to be undertaken. Unfortunately, teachers who do this instinctively frequently pick low-level considerations for emphasis ('Don't forget to underline the title', 'I want to see plenty of good adjectives', 'Divide it properly into paragraphs'). Third, by our reception of work we can help to diminish the anxiety – destructive of good work – that comes from uncertainty about just what the teacher is really looking for and concerned about. Fourth, we can avoid giving over-rigid and over-demanding specifications that will inhibit growth and originality of treatment. Fifth, we can devise simple activities that will focus attention on one particular aspect of writing.

Such activities, which isolate one part of the process, are inevitably artificial. They are important not for themselves but as a way of signalling the kind of attention which is to be given to the next piece of writing. Some very brief suggestions follow, that could be adapted to the particular conditions of a writing programme.

FINDING AND REALIZING IDEAS

i) Write on the board a simple sentence like 'The horse went over the bridge'. Ask pupils to visualize this in their mind's eye. Quick questions about each element: what colour is *your* horse? how big? on his own or with a rider? is he pulling anything? old or young? *How* does he go? Describe his movements. What kind of bridge? over what? Establish that on the simplest basis they have created quite different scenes.

ii) Distribute copies of a banal, inconclusive story outline, e.g. 'My friend got hold of an old box. His father wanted him to throw it away, but he wouldn't. A man saw it and wanted it.' Ask pupils to write below the story questions which need to be answered but which the story doesn't tell. Share and consider these. Ask two or three to re-tell the story adding details that will make it coherent and bring it to an end.

iii) Produce three objects (e.g. an old hat, a small bell and a family photograph, or a pair of boots, a bar of soap and a half-finished picture). Tell children they have five minutes in which to think of a story in which each of those three objects plays an important part. (You may wish to suggest that they think of *who* is involved, *where*, *when* and *why*.) Then invite pupils in pairs to tell their stories to each other and to discuss the results.

iv) Collaborative writing in pairs. Ask couples to produce a short story in which they take it in turns to write one sentence each, aiming to produce a final text that might have been composed by a single person.

v) Divide class into groups of about four, and give each group a head-and-shoulders photograph of a person to be the central character in an incident. Each person in the group is to add one detail to the character (has a limp, collects stamps, lives in a caravan, hates children). When these are forthcoming, each is to explain how this feature came to exist and how it affects the character's life.

DEVELOPING SEQUENCE AND STRUCTURE

i) Give pairs or groups a comic strip story in which the frames have been cut up separately, and ask them to put them back in order. Discuss how they know what the correct sequence is.

ii) Similar exercise (a) with a short story, cut into separate paragraphs or other sections and (b) with a sequential piece of non-fiction (e.g. instructions for carrying out a process). What similarities and what differences between the two tasks?

iii) Suggesting that a writer organizes material so that it can be easily followed by readers, try one or both of the following:

   a) Distribute copies of a badly-structured piece which students are to improve (try to use the description of a process with which they will already be familiar).

   b) Give out a story or non-fiction passage in which key sentences (i.e. those which involve a shift in direction or organization) have been omitted. Ask pupils to write in their versions of the missing sentences and then to compare them with partner's.

iv) Divide class into groups, and give each a news story and an editorial referring to it. Ask groups to make notes on the different organization of each passage and relate this to the different function they think it is to serve. Groups to report back to the rest of the class.

v) Take a wide topic (pets or transport or explorers) and ask groups to find different ways of classifying these (with younger children, build up lists of examples on the board first). Consider the effects of dividing transport, say, into different groups according to:

   land, sea, air, amphibious
   past, present, future
   animal power, steam, petrol or diesel, electric, rocket
   fast, slow, etc.

FITTING THE AUDIENCE

i) Discussion to evoke the concept of audience and awareness that different works are aimed at different audiences.
Consider which television programmes or magazines are
most popular with the group, and ask why certain others
are not watched or read by any of them.

ii) Divide class into groups of four and ask each person in the
group to choose one of head-teacher, parent, best
friend of same sex, boy or girl friend of opposite sex. Tell
them they are all to imagine having committed a serious
breach of school discipline, details of which you give. In
their groups, each in turn is to tell the story of this
incident, but to a different audience (the one they have
chosen: head-teacher, parent or friend). Follow with a
class discussion of the differences which changing the
audience made to the narration.

iii) Examine some of the following examples of written work
which distinguish between audiences in different respects:
   a) A section of a story written for the class's age group
      and one intended for children several years younger.
   b) Description of an animal from a Lawrence Durrell
      travel book and from an encyclopaedia.
   c) An extract from a historical novel and from a history
      textbook. In discussion, establish the connection
      between audience and function.

iv) Using a short story which the class has been reading, ask
them in groups to prepare a brief retelling of the story in
language that would make it intelligible and interesting to
children four or five years younger than they are.

v) Using a newspaper report of a person killed in a local fire,
road accident or other disaster, ask members of each
group to prepare notes on how the facts would be
presented (a) in a formal police report (b) in a letter from
a close relative to another (c) in an article using the death
to complain about fire precautions or road safety (d) on
local radio.

MAKING A CHOICE

It may be helpful to direct attention to the ways in which different patterns in writing convey different shades of meaning. Children's early writing seems dull and flat because we cannot hear the inner voice they *think* they are transcribing. They have to learn how to produce particular effects by shifting the stress or selecting the precise word to change the emphasis.

i) Put on the board a simple sentence like, 'The butcher could see the tree swaying'. Ask pupils to suggest places in which the word *only* could be inserted. Then ask them to explain the different emphasis given by 'only the butcher' or 'could only see' or 'the only tree'. Is there any difference between 'Only the butcher' and 'The butcher only', or between 'the tree only swaying' and 'the tree swaying only'?

ii) *a*) Ask students to rearrange sentences, without changing the actual words used, in order to create particular effects, e.g. 'She saw a deadly black tarantula on the white pillow only a few inches from her eye as she awoke' (build up tension). 'He ran out of the room and down the stairs through the door into the street and out of sight' (avoid monotony).

    b) Ask them to combine sentences in different ways to produce varied emphasis, e.g. Join 'Harry would not go to the theatre with us' and 'He was too busy'; to emphasize the reason for his behaviour; to suggest that this always happened in such circumstances; to imply some doubt about the reason.

iii) Examine ambiguous headlines ('General flies back to front', 'Dog in bed asks divorce') discussing reasons for range of meanings. Ask pairs to work on one or more of the following, each writing a different news item under the same headline to indicate the variety of possible interpretations:

    '20 stone organist misses the city hall' (*Hull Daily Mail*).

'Spotted man wanted for questioning' (*Hackney Gazette*).

'Horse girl suspended by head' (*Daily Telegraph*).

iv) a) Consider the different emotional emphasis of words which refer to the same thing, e.g. the differences in association between thoroughbred, horse, nag, palfrey. Ask pupils to arrange a collection of words in three columns, according to whether they are neutral or generally approving or disapproving equivalents, or give one and ask for suggestions for the other two, e.g.

Approving	Neutral	Disapproving
Mansion		
	Ship	
		Mob
Statesman		
	Clothing	
		Glutton

   b) Ask pairs to produce matched descriptions of the same scene to create opposing impressions because of the loaded terms used, e.g. a gipsy encampment as seen by an admiring artist and by the angry farmer on whose land they have camped without permission.

v) Rehandling different kinds of language to make them more effective.

   a) Vague or open sentences to be made more vivid or precise, e.g. The officer seemed cross at the sailor's behaviour. The lady looked tired as she came into the room.

   b) Complex language to be simplified, e.g. He proffered his assistance with commendable promptitude. I cannot contemplate with equanimity the prevarications you articulate.

Children often enjoy decoding pedantic versions of proverbs (refrain from taking a census of the progeny of the feathered fowl prior to their emergence from the sheathing calcareous encrustation).

c) Avoiding clichés, the journalistic (my blood froze, a ghastly hush, a sickening thud) or the genteel (bereavement, purveyor, financially embarrassed).

The sense of oneself as writer

It is crucial for success that children should develop a sense of themselves as writers. This sense can be defined in different ways: as coming to see the whole world of experience as a subject for writing, or as awareness that writing is to make a series of deliberate choices. Harold Rosen has argued that the essential ability is being able to represent to oneself the situational context for any piece of writing, including the intended readers. The writer, that is,

> must carry out a procedure of self-editing, of arresting, reorganizing and adjusting his message for his absent audience. He will be unable to do this unless he can *internalize* his audience.[17]

Young writers' sense of audience has to be balanced by the accompanying awareness of themselves as capable of telling a story, explaining a process, discussing a process.

In particular there is the question of *voice*: the way in which we hear what we have to say, define our stance towards the subject and the audience. Donald Graves has called voice 'the imprint of the person on the piece of writing. The way in which a writer chooses, selects and organizes information towards the writer's own intention'.[18] What we do not fully understand is how this ability is developed, and how that inner voice dictates to us in forms that are appropriate to the written language rather than to speech. Early writing seems to be a direct capturing of the spoken word, and often embodies features that try to convey in pallid symbols the excitement of what is heard in the head '5 – 4 – 3 – 2 – 1 – Blast off!'

'Vroom, vroom, here they come!' 'It's a goal!' Words are written in capitals or are underlined several times to suggest the necessary emphasis. Preliminary talk (or continuing talk) is important at this stage because the voice has to be found orally and then realized on paper before it vanishes again.

Because progress depends on a developing sense of what it is that authors do, the growth of the personal voice in writing seems dependent – however ironical it may sound – on a process of trying on other voices. It is the pupil who learns to write in various styles, who can consciously or subconsciously imitate the authors most recently read, who seems also to develop the awareness of having an individual way of writing. There is clearly an element of play in this process. While being perfectly aware that the teacher is the 'real' audience, children can simultaneously imagine themselves writing for a journalist's mass public or the listeners to a radio soap opera. They can parody clearly marked styles, writing 'in the manner of' authors recently read. When they are doing work of this kind it helps them to become more aware of how different voices sound. We do not know how far this is dependent on particular kinds of reading, or how far good writers read 'better' than (or differently from) poor writers, but varying assumed voices in this way seems to develop the awareness of increasingly subtle differences from which a personal style of writing emerges.

We want our children to feel 'This is me speaking, in my authentic voice, not someone else's' and yet for the writing also to be distinct from speech, appropriate to the chosen written mode. So much of our practice, though, makes it hard for them. We may impose our own strident voice and damp out theirs. We may destroy their confidence by ill-judged criticism. Worst of all, we may mock the experimentation by which they are reaching towards another voice. The clichés they use, the apparent sentimentality or sensationalism, are often their first shy attempts to try something new by borrowing attitudes in which they feel safer.

A 15-year-old girl who casts herself in the role of forsaken lover turns instinctively to pop song lyrics to help her convey her feelings. Her poem 'I'll never forget you' begins:

> I miss you most in the evenings,
> No arms to hold me tight,
> No warm brown eyes gaze into mine,
> No lips kiss me good night.
>
> I sit alone in the evenings,
> And play our song again.
> It's over a month since you left me,
> But I still feel the pain.

The reference to playing our song is significant. The less articulate let the singers speak for them; to adapt the singer's mode, however impoverished, is a step towards personal expression. The song acts as a cloak to prevent the girl's feelings from being too nakedly exposed. To arrest her at this stage would be to reduce the chances for her to attempt an authentic response. We can be so devoted to the concept of originality that we see imitation as a vice rather than as a sign of potential growth.

Some impression of learning by 'trying on' different voices can be gained by looking at some extracts from the work of an able fourth year girl in a large comprehensive school just outside Hull. In class and on her own she has been reading Dylan Thomas's *Portrait of the Artist as a Young Dog*, poems and prose by Lawrence, Winifred Holtby's *South Riding*, John Wyndham's *The Chrysalids*, some paraphases of Old English poems, and Thurber's 'The Secret Life of Walter Mitty'. In written work, she is sometimes asked by the teacher to use her reading as a starting point; sometimes she is influenced less consciously. Consider the different voices through which she speaks in these openings of a number of pieces from that year, shown in the sequence in which they were written.

The Race

The next morning Dan, Sidney and I left George asleep, exhausted after running on Rhossilli sands half the night. As we got breakfast ready we talked anxiously about Brazell and Skully and how we could keep away from them for even a day. All our high hopes for a wonderful fortnight of freedom were dashed by the meeting with the two bullies.

'Hallo, boys', came a voice behind us, which made us start. It was Brazell. 'Up a bit late, aren't we? Skully and I have been up since five o'clock.'

The Best Afternoon in the Whole Summer

With the stirrings of a breeze, the light is dappled
On Classroom desks.
Shouts of delight from the wide, green sportsfield
Fall on deaf ears.
Silence.
The teacher drones with the traffic at the crossroads
His pupils watching
The classroom clock

Sarah Burton

At the opening of the book Sarah has just come to Kiplington from a large London school to become headmistress of the school there. She gets the job because of her shrewd intelligence and the fact that she was born locally herself, and became a success in her field. Her appointment is opposed by only one governor of the school, Robin Carne.

Sarah is a small red-headed woman who believes that one should get success through knowing what one wants and working to achieve it. Her motto comes from a Spanish proverb: 'Take what you want', said God, 'Take it, and pay for it.' She has never met any opposition, either physical or emotional, to her theory, throughout her life, and believes that, at thirty-nine, life is not going to start opposing her wishes.

The 'Sun' and the 'Guardian'

The fact that the *Sun* report took up a third of a page, and the *Guardian* report was a short one in 'News in Brief' tells me that the *Sun* aims to please readers about events in the lives of people like themselves, rather than report upon events of world-wide importance. Readers of the *Guardian* want a newspaper that deals with important issues of the day, and gives just the plain facts of minor events.

A Speech

Ladies, may I ask how you manage to be here tonight? Could it be that you come after a long struggle with yourself? Are you sitting here now wondering whether your husbands have remembered to turn off the oven, whether the children are in bed yet? If so, you can satisfy yourselves with the knowledge that you are living up to society's expectations of you.

Untitled Story

The roars of the crowd grew louder. Through determined, half-shut eyes the world-famous athlete saw the finishing line ahead. Supremely confident, with the rest of the field trailing at a long distance she crossed it. Ann Peterson the coach was coming up with a crowd of television interviewers, and over her head commentators' voices came over the loudspeakers, announcing the time of the new world record...

'Four fifteen', barked Miss Finch. 'Try harder next time, Biddy.' Biddy straightened up and saw her friends coming towards her.

'Hard luck, Biddy!' they chorused. Someone handed her a cardigan, and she took it, adjusting her glasses at the same time. Savagely she thought she would do better next time, it was just bad luck.

My Experience of Shakespeare's Plays

Although until last year I had never actually read any of the plays, I had read, when I was about nine, Lamb's *Tales from Shakespeare* which did not mean very much to me. However, last year when our English class read *Macbeth* I already knew the plot fairly well, and some lines, as a teacher at my Junior School told us the story and encouraged us to watch the play on television.

I have also read *The Tempest* and watched it on television. I find it a lot easier to understand Shakespeare if I have read the play beforehand. I saw *A Winter's Tale* on television, and kept up with it as I had a vague idea about the plot, but when I went to see *Henry IV* at the theatre I was completely lost as to what was happening several times!

When we look at even these brief extracts, we are struck by the variety of written styles that this girl displays in English (the variety is much wider, of course, if we also look at her work in other subjects). There are differences according to mode and function – story, description, poem, critique, speech – and also according to the envisaged audience: herself, an imagined hall full of listeners, friends in the class and particularly the teacher. In addition, though, different poems and stories written during the year differ in style. A number of pieces are written in the first person, but the 'I' is a very different person in each. It is interesting that she seems so much more confident in her handling of fiction of quite different styles (getting inside the Mittyish fantasies of Biddie and having a stab at being a boy) than she does when writing in her own person. The language in which she discusses Shakespeare is not only limited, but sounds naive by comparison. This is frequently the case with able young writers. They are able to be more confident within an assumed persona than in revealing themselves, and stylistically it is much easier to write a pastiche of someone else's distinctive style than to trust one's own rather hesitant voice. When we look at the first pieces of Joanna's work in the fifth year, though, we are conscious of how far she has developed in twelve months. The increased confidence, and the willingness to trust her own voice are marked.

The teacher as organizer of the writing process

What does the teacher do while the pupils are actually writing? A few years ago the answer would have been clear: spend the time marking the work done by another class. Now, with the shift of emphasis from end-product to the writing process, teachers are much more likely to intervene while composing is going on, offering help at the point where it is needed, rather than waiting for the assignment to be 'finished'. Like most generalizations, this is not an invariable rule. On occasions teachers may decide that the most valuable strategy is to sit and write with the children on the same topic, and then to compare responses with them. Nevertheless the norm is for teachers to be active while writing goes on.

Sometimes activity can be misguided. It may be a kind of royal progress dispensing bland approval ('Lovely, Donald', 'Oh that *is* nice, Samantha'). It may be distracting, as a pupil's work reminds the teacher of a point that should have been emphasized ('Now listen, everybody, what did I say about paragraphs?'). It may start too soon, ignoring the need for a quiet period, in which most children can actually get started, before individuals can be offered help.

Underlying everything which the teacher does is the need to distinguish between the different processes for which help is being offered (and, indeed, the processes where it may be better *not* to help) and to diagnose the particular needs of an individual. If we use terms like preparation – incubation – illumination – resolution, for instance, the teacher may wish to intervene quite differently in the first and last processes, but to keep clear of the individual, unconscious ones.

One of the most sobering experiences students or young teachers undergo is to take a lesson they have observed succeeding in the hands of a more experienced teacher and to find that it fails in their own. The reason for the failure is rarely in the material or plan of the lesson; it is almost always the organization that collapses. The more choice and flexibility children have in their time for writing, the more organization and structure is needed – quite the reverse of many students' assumptions.

Consider the simplest writing situation: a mixed-ability group who have been talking in groups about their memories of quarrels, and are now going to write about such an incident, completing this by the end of the double period. Some of the group will be reluctant, some will quietly want to get away with the minimum, one or two may be disruptive, a few are keen to get started, one wants to impress the teacher, and so on. What are the chief organizational problems for the teacher here, and in most other writing situations?

a) Getting the work launched. We know from the Teacher Education Project that the danger moments in a lesson are those when there is a change of activity, and the shift from talking to writing is particularly difficult, because knowing what the first words will be takes time. There is a key period of about five minutes until most pupils have begun, and different teachers tackle this in different ways. Some expect work to be done in silence. This is difficult to maintain, though perhaps not more difficult than deciding how much talk, at what volume and for how long shall be permitted. Some teachers 'talk into the writing': they continue speaking almost hypnotically about the subject, not to convey information but to suppress other distractions. One teacher I know always played quiet music at this point. The essential principle is not to become absorbed in helping individuals until this early period is over and most of them are writing.

b) Helping the reluctant to begin. Some ideas for getting students started were described on pages 125–9. Shivering on the brink of a blank page is inhibiting for the individual and possibly distracting for others nearby. The teacher may talk with the student to identify a possible starting point, provide supplementary materials to spark off an idea, offer a written model to work from, arrange for two students to collaborate, reframe the assignment, or even ask the student to try jotting down *why* it seems hard to get started.

c) Deciding on the priorities: who needs help most and how can it be given? This diagnostic and consultancy role is discussed further on pages 164–7.

d) Encouraging rewriting. This is considered more fully on pages 167–76.

e) Bringing the work to a close. Even if a time limit is given, it is idle to imagine that all members of a group will finish neatly at the same moment. The teacher needs to think beforehand about what will be done with the early finishers (revision at teacher's directions? sharing with one another to read and discuss? completely different work – reading or a workcard?) and what will happen to those who are still in mid-stream at the end (keeping the work to finish at home? giving it in for reading, but finishing later? simply abandoning it?). The habit of writing up to the bell is rarely a good one. It is often better to move back from individual work to a group activity for the last few minutes. It may simply be the teacher summing up and collecting the work, or it may be a discussion about children's reactions to the assignment on which they have been engaged, or it may be listening to the work done by one or two of them, or it may be hearing a poem or extract on the same theme. If pupils *are* asked to read their work – or to let someone else read it – then the teacher will have asked them beforehand; nothing is more damaging than the public request to read followed by an embarrassed or truculent refusal.

f) Setting homework. Homework provides the elastic for

most written assignments. The commonest teacher instruction seems to be 'Finish off at home'. Certainly, for reasons already indicated in this chapter, it is rarely helpful to expect all of a piece to be written outside school. Homework might be used more often, though, as an opportunity for *beginning* work and gathering ideas, making notes, starting to draft – with the main stage of the writing coming during the following lesson. The students have longer for ideas to germinate, and the teacher has more time to concentrate with them on the writing process itself.

The teacher as consultant

Who most needs my attention? What kind of assistance shall I offer? These are difficult diagnostic decisions. Inexperienced teachers frequently assume that the children who need help are those who put their hands up. Unfortunately these tend to include the fussy, the attention-seekers and the troublesome. Those who do *not* raise their hands include those who are afraid of exposing their inadequacy, those who do not realize that their work is going badly wrong, the shy and the superior who feel loftily above help. A major organizational problem is sharing out a strictly limited amount of teacher time. Some find it necessary to keep records to ensure that over a period all members of a class have a reasonable share of attention. Who gets helped first? It will probably be those who have been unable to get started, but the treatment will vary according to whether the teacher feels they are being lazy, perfectionist, insecure or simply slow. Pupils who rush on carelessly may be told to stop at the end of five lines, check what they have written, and then to ask for the teacher's opinion and approval before continuing. Fussy pupils may be challenged to be more independent: 'Your last work was fine, so let's see whether you can work for half-an-hour without asking a question of me or anyone else.' Pupils who are stuck may be helped by seeing what others have written. In fact, the most appropriate form of help may often be bringing two students together for 'cross-pollination', or forming a small group to tackle a shared problem together.

Observation in many classrooms suggests that when younger children put up their hands or try in other ways to attract the teacher's attention, much of the help they need is at a very low level from the instructional point of view. They want reassurance ('Do we have to ...?' 'Is this right?') and to avoid error ('How do you spell ...?' 'What is the word for ...?'). Somehow the teacher has to pre-empt these demands (by insisting on the use of dictionaries, by encouraging mutual help between children, by allowing individuals only one question in a session). Otherwise they snowball. On occasions, half the pupils in a class can be inactive, simply waiting for the teacher's attention. And from the teacher's point of view giving help at this level reduces, or even eliminates, the more important consultancy work.

The chief purpose of consultation is to help students to know and to express what they already 'know'. Set to write on the subject 'Accident', after hearing Bill Naughton's 'Spit Nolan' and seeing photographs of car accidents, a second-year girl of below average ability produced this:

The Accident
One day my friend and I was going away with her mother in the car. Her mother has fair hair, brown eyes. She is 6'5" and she works at the Spar. We were on our way to Aberdeen when we had an accident. It was all right till we came to this corner and went round this corner to fast and goes straight towards this fence. We went through the fence and into the field and the car is a right of. Fiona's mother was killed and Fiona and I were alright. So the police took Fiona home and she lived with her father till she was old enough to get married. The end.[19]

This is a typical piece of flat, sequential writing; largely unfelt, and with little sense of audience. Once work of this kind is 'completed', there is often a block about revising it, but it is easier to intervene during the writing. If you had reached this girl at mid-point in her description of the incident, what would you have said in order to help? We can exemplify four distinct strategies here. Would you simply exchange memories and impressions about accidents in the hope that creating more vivid impressions in her mind might increase the vividness of the writing? Or would you concentrate on realizing the impression within the story? (How did you feel when the car went off the road? What was the car like after it went through the fence?) Or would you emphasize the structure and narrative style? (Why might it be better not to use the word 'accident' until later? Which sentence do we really not need? Should we be told why Fiona's mother was driving so fast?) Or would you concentrate on getting her to tell the story to a specific audience first? (Look, I don't know where 'this' corner and 'this' fence are; you'll have to help me to understand what went on.) In the abstract, no one of these approaches, sharing, realizing, focusing, stressing audience, is necessarily better than another, but a teacher who knows the pupils will try to select the one that seems best for the situation.

A secondary purpose of consultation is to diagnose those features of language use with which the individual may need help; possibly to offer it on the spot, or later to a group of pupils. In 'The Accident' there are more important matters than the shifts between past and present tenses, but these might be picked up later. Frequently, however, children reveal in writing a need which can best be tackled at the moment they need it. First attempts to give the actual words spoken by characters suggest that the child is ready for quotation marks, and that they can be learned because they are needed rather than as an artificial exercise.

There does seem to be evidence that such help in developing and organizing ideas is associated with improvement in writing ability.[20] Our instinctive ideas of guidance are being shaped under the rather grandiose title of 'the process-conference approach' in the USA. One quoted example shows a series of six brief conferences, over a period of time, with a boy named Jerry who is anxious to write a piece about sharks. His teacher begins by probing his experience and interests and goes on to nudge him towards possible sources of information. It is the fourth conference before she sees the first connected draft:

Jerry: Well, here's the first shot. What do you think?

Ms Putnam: You have a good start, Jerry. Look at these first four paragraphs. Tell me which one makes you feel as if you were there.

Jerry: This one here, the fourth one, where I tell about two kids who are out trying to harpoon a shark.

Ms Putnam: Don't you think this is the one that will interest the reader most? Start right off with it.[21]

By the sixth conference, they are discussing what can be omitted, what examples should be added, and what kinds of rewriting are necessary before the final copy is prepared. Ideas of revision are considered further in the next section.[22]

Encouraging rewriting

In English classrooms, revision is often narrowly defined as reading through what has been written and putting right the mistakes. Very little time is given for this, and it is almost universally unpopular ('When I've finished, I hate to have to read it'). Rewriting is a little researched and little taught skill. It often carries overtones of failure or even punishment ('Very poor. Repeat this work'). And yet we know from our own experience and from that of professional authors that writing demands rewriting, that it is an essential part of the process.

One analysis of empirical studies on the teaching of writing found that one of the two factors associated with improvement in students' work was revision. Methods of guiding rewriting varied, but 'the revision process itself, which gives students an opportunity to make immediate application of suggestions for improvement, is critical in improving student writing'.[23] If we believe that writing is frequently a 'discovery method', that we learn what we mean in the act of writing, then it is clear that the flash of illumination, the awareness of what we 'really' want to say, the apprehension of the appropriate structure, may come late as well as early. When this happens, we have to go back and reorganize the work. It is the failure to do this that we so often see in the stories of younger children. The shifts of the protagonist from 'he' to 'I', the changes of tense from past to present, are simply the more obvious linguistic features revealing more profound changes of direction.

There seem to be two difficulties for the teacher. First, children think of their writing as completed at the first attempt; once on paper it appears fixed and unchangeable. In part this is because all the other texts they see – stories, letters, blackboard notes, magazines – are finished products. They have no experience of the rehandling that goes into the production of these, and so rewriting as a concept has no significance. Second, we often confuse two processes by lumping them together in the term 'revision'. There is the rewriting, rehandling, reorganizing of the text, much of which may go on *during* the writing, and which involves making new choices about sequence, developing or cutting sections, phraseology, tone and so on. Then there is the editing of the completed text, a final stage in the work, which tidies it for the reader, ensuring that it is acceptable in the mechanical sense: that the syntax, spelling and punctuation are correct. Only the author can rewrite; any educated reader can edit (and, indeed, the marking of some teachers is simply reduced to editing).

All children need help in learning to revise in both of these two senses. In particular they need help in distancing themselves from what they have written: to see revising as a kind of interaction with themselves, talking to the person they have created through the words on the page. Children who begin everything ('The big match', 'The fishing trip', 'A visit to London') 'We got up and had egg and bacon for breakfast', and who reach the supposed subject in the last paragraph, need to learn about selection by becoming more of a real audience to themselves. Most of them have to learn about rewriting from help initially given by the teacher, and this is much more effective if it is offered during the writing rather than after it. Graves has shown that with appropriate help even very young children can acquire the necessary skills of revision,[24] and they are equally important for fluent and less fluent older children.

Aided rewriting in the early stages can be a real means of helping less able pupils to engage more effectively in writing. Consider this work by an 11-year-old boy at a rural comprehensive school outside Hull. He had just been transferred from a remedial group, where much of his work had been on exercises, to a first year mixed-ability class. The pupils were writing about imaginary experiences after being shipwrecked on an island. His eventual title was 'The encanted island'. 'Encanted' was written above two previous attempts at another word (marvellous?), and 'island' was tried twice. He wrote:

It was a windy day in december we crash into a rok

At this point he stuck and was helped by his teacher. The next draft ran:

The enchanted island

In Was a windy day me and my crew crash into a rock and the boat began to sink all the crew drowned, and I got on a bit of the ship and float to a Island did not drowned I got on a

After discussing this with the teacher and making one or two marks on the writing he produced this third opening:

> The enchanted island
> It was a windy day and the sea was ruff and wild and the ship crashed into some rocks and water came overboard, the ship sunk very fast all the crew did not get far away from the ship and i did and the crew got suck under with the ship and I got away on a dingy and I came to a island.

At this stage he is explaining why the ship crashed and what happened with some degree of vividness. The important thing is that he has also been freed to push forward more confidently with the narrative. The third draft runs to four pages. The final illustrated version (the beginning of which is not significantly changed from the previous draft) is six pages long.[25]

Rewriting may do more than improve the quality of expression. If on occasions we only discover what we feel in the process of writing it, then rewriting may be essential to convey that new awareness. Some indication of what this means can be gained by examining two versions of an account written by a quite able third-year girl. The original piece, entitled 'The worst place I've been', was a tidily presented description of visiting an elderly relative in a geriatric ward. The introduction explains the circumstances, and how 'I wasn't looking forward to it at all in fact I was dreading it.' This is the way in which the occasion is described.

> After school I met mum to go up to the hospital. We followed the signs to the geriateric ward. As soon as we went into the ward I went cold. I looked around at all the old womens faces. They looked suprised to see me I supose they don't see many children. As I walk down the ward towards the chair where the old lady was sitting I felt all there eyes were on me. My spine qwithered. I hated it I wanted to turn around and ran out, but rose was looking forward to see

me so I went on I felt awkward and embarresed.

Rose looked very unhappy. She told us how she did not like the nurses as she thought they were all very bad tempered and unpatient. She told us how one of the nurses put a piece of pastry in front of her for her to play with. Rose felt very degraded as she used to run and own a hotel and was a very good cook. I felt sorry for her. We said goodbye and I started walking towards the door. All the old ladys eyes were still on me again. I walked a bit faster till I reached the door. It was cold outside. I felt relieved that we were out of that horrid building.

Although this is clearly written, it is also rather flat. There is so much concentration on the girl herself and on her feelings that we get little sense of the ward. There is nothing to indicate why this should be the *worst* place she had ever been. As readers we are told of her emotions, but not helped to share them. The rewritten version is much more effective. Not only is the life of the ward much more precisely and vividly conveyed, the writer has also realized that some of the professed feelings of the original draft were a sham. The second draft concentrates on the differences between what she imagined the place would be like and the actuality, between her own instinctive feelings as a young outsider and those of the patients and nurses. The focus of attention keeps shifting. Significantly she alters the title to 'The place that changed my mind', and shifts the conclusion from 'I hope I never have to go there again' to 'for many people its lovely as they love the company'. The redrafted version, twice the length of the original one, reads like this:

Monday after school I met mum at the hospital entrance.

I could just imagine what is was going to be like old ladies staring with open mouths shouting things their brain had no control over. And me standing there feeling very embarras.

While following the signs to the geriateric ward, I kept thinking of what it was going to be like. We both entered the pink painted ward.

At first I thought it was exactly how I had imagined.

There were old ladies playing with jigsaw pieces and drawing indifinable pictures. You could tell they enjoyed watching the colours appearing on the paper. They were content.

The lady with the jigsaw puzzle looked at me and laughed, as she put a piece of the jig-saw in her mouth. She wanted attention and she soon got it. A nurse who had seen her came rushing towards her.

A turned to walk towards Rose listening at the same time to hear what the nurse was saying.

The nurse's vioce was sturn as she told the old lady about the dangers of swollowing things. What a waste of time telling her that was. If she wanted to eat it she would no matter what the nurse said.

Mum was already talking to Rose so I walked quietly to get a chair.

Rose started asking how school was and what lessons I did not like and lots off other things that I wasn't really listening too. I was too busy watching the old lady down the corridoor. Now she was throwing the jig-saw around and laughing uncontrolably at the nurse who was trying to quiet her down. I laughed to myself. I wondered what she would do next.

My attention was taken from the old lady and zoomed onto what Rose was talking about.

She told us how she did not like the nurses. She said they were bossy and very unpatient.

Her shaking hand pointed to a nurse who was loading a trolley full of cups of tea and biscuits.

'She', Rose said bitterly, 'Put a piece of pastry, no bigger than a walnut in front of me as if she wants me to play with it.'

Rose was so angry because she used to run and own a hotel and is a very good cook.

'I hate it here', she said sadly. I felt sorry for her. I am very fond of her.

A ginger haired nurse came briskley down the corridor ringing a big bell. We had to go. So we said good bye to Rose and went.

As we went out of the door I could hear the old lady laughing. A piecing laugh like a witch. But I was wrong about this place it wasn't as bad as I thought. They were all harmless, like a bunch of small kids. They just needed patience.[26]

If revision is to take place during the writing process itself then it will, of course, depend on the expectations created during all English lessons. If work is normally received and marked as a finished product, then it is unlikely that children will see much point in spending more time on what has already been assessed. If work is usually given to be handed in at the end of the period, then the child's cry of 'Finished!' means just that. We have seen from children's comments that when they are given a longer period of time and a degree of freedom about when the writing is done, many of them not only enjoy the work more but are prepared to spend more time and effort on improving it. The teacher can only suggest revision during the writing process if the conditions permit (not if the writing is being done in an immaculate exercise book), if the notion of redrafting is accepted and if the individual is responsive to the need. There are several ways in which children can be helped to overcome an initial antipathy for rewriting.

a) Breaking down the assumption that what we begin to

write will also be the finished version. Pupils who are forced to write sequentially in a tidy exercise book are faced with the task of simultaneously composing and structuring in the best possible way. As adults we rarely do this. When I am writing an article, I get down ideas on to paper with little concern for weighing my words; when I get stuck I go on to another point; if a sudden idea comes then I jot it down. Later comes the juggling, the deletion, the rephrasing, the scissors-and-sellotape process. There I often leave it for a while, so that I can return to it with a critical, detached mind, which often prompts new ideas as the final draft is hammered out. If we are preparing children for writing in the real world, then we should be encouraging some such process as this. They have to overcome fear of the messy page. They need to work on paper and to be encouraged to chop it up or to mark it in different colours, to use arrows and to put alternatives in the margins. If work has to be done in exercise books, then some teachers ask for the left-hand page to be used for rough drafting and the right-hand page for the revised version (or divide each page into two columns of equal width).[27] When we go round the class discussing work, then some of our questions should be prompting reorganization of what has been written: Couldn't this be told in flash-back? Which of these points should come first to catch the reader's interest? Don't these two ideas really need to be together? How about putting in an actual example?

b) In the early stages, working with them as a group on editing. They can be given drafts of material which require expansion, rearrangement or clarification, or where the language is clumsy, lacking in vividness or rambling. After working on these individually, they can compare notes, and groups can work towards an agreed 'polished' version. At first these passages may be deliberately prepared to emphasize particular editorial skills, but eventually groups should be asked to deal with their own work in the same way. It helps if photocopies can be made, so that several students can simultaneously be editing the same piece. In choosing subjects for writing, we may encourage them to experiment with a task or technique that makes rehandling almost inevitable: first attempts at interior monologue, a sequence of working instructions, a set of memories about a person or place at different times, a reasoned argument for a particular point of view.

c) Introducing them to the way in which professional authors redraft their work. Weaker writers in school often seem to imagine that 'real' writers know just what they are going to say before they say it, and this notion inhibits their own writing. Classes can examine the successive drafts by which poets and novelists came to the final form of their works. Useful material of this kind, including facsimiles of manuscripts are collected in volumes like *The Poet's Craft*.[28] William Sansom's *The Birth of a Story* describes at a relatively simple level how a short story 'No smoking on the apron' came to be, with photocopied pages of typescript and manuscript accompanying explanations of why certain changes were made.[29] The purpose of such work is not simply to let children see that writers *do* have to revise but to help them to understand the reasons for the revision. Students who examine successive drafts of part of a James Joyce short story or a Wilfred Owen poem, for example, do not always agree that the final version is the best, but they do tend to agree on what it is that the revisions are achieving.

d) Providing the kind of audience that gives purpose to redrafting. The notion of 'publishing' work is dealt with more fully in a separate section (see pages 204–10) but here we are simply concerned with the incentive that an audience can give for revision. Enjoyment and encouragement, of course, are as important as critical suggestions. 'What did you particularly enjoy about this?' or 'Which part seemed best?' can be as helpful as 'How could this be improved?'. Even the simplest mode – work being read aloud by the author to the teacher or a group, followed by discussion – frequently leads to awareness of the kinds of change that are needed. Children can be encouraged to operate in groups of four or five, circulating their work around the others with a blank sheet attached, on which each reader adds suggestions for improvement, so that the work returns with four or five different sets of comments.

References

1   See Frank Whitehead, *Creative Experiment*, Writing and the Teacher, London, Chatto & Windus, 1970.

2   Ronald Blythe, 'The Mechanics of Magic', *The Times Educational Supplement*, 12 March 1976.

3   Richard Potts, 'Diligence and Inspiration', *The Times Educational Supplement*, 25 June 1976.

4   Cornelia Jones and Olivia R. Way, *British Children's Authors*, Interviews at home, Chicago, American Library Association, 1976.

5   ibid., p. 169.

6   ibid., p. 7.

7   ibid., p. 170.

8   ibid., p. 130.

9   ibid., p. 97.

10   ibid., p. 147.

11   ibid., pp. 78–9.

12   ibid., pp. 132, 50, 58.

13   Janet Emig, *The Composing Processes of Twelfth Graders*, Urbana, Illinois, NCTE, 1971; D.H. Graves, 'An examination of the writing processes of seven year old children', *Research in the Teaching of English*, 1975, 9, pp. 227–41; Charles R. Cooper and Lee Odell, *Research on Composing*, Urbana, Illinois, NCTE, 1978.

14   'Craft and Art', *The English Magazine*, Spring 1981,

No. 6, pp. 4–10.

15 See the examples in *Becoming Our Own Experts*, Studies in language and learning made by the Talk Workshop Group at Vauxhall Manor School, 1982.

16 James Hartley, *The Psychology of Written Communication*, London, Kogan Page, 1980.

17 Harold Rosen, 'Written language and the sense of audience', *Educational Research*, June 1973, 15, No. 3, p. 180.

18 'Donald Graves on Writing', *The English Magazine*, Autumn 1981, No. 8, p. 5.

19 Quoted by David Northcroft, 'Pupils' writing: product, process and evaluation', *English in Education*, Summer 1979, 13, No. 2, pp. 16–17.

20 Some of the research is summarized in Betty Bamberg, 'Composition instruction does make a difference', *Research in the Teaching of English*, 1978, 12, No. 1, pp. 47–59.

21 Donald H. Graves, *Balance the Basics: Let Them Write*, New York, Ford Foundation, 1978, pp. 19–21.

22 Also see Peter Medway, *Finding a Language*, Writers and Readers, 1980.

23 Bamberg, op. cit., p. 50.

24 D. H. Graves, 'What children show us about revision', *Language Arts*, 1979, 56, No. 3, p. 312. See also Jenny Gubb, 'Back to the Drawing Board', *English in Education*, Summer 1983, 17, No. 2.

25 I am grateful to Mike Smith of Howden School for this example.

26 My thanks to Peter Medway, who gave permission for me to use this example.

27 Fuller details, with some interesting examples of successive drafts, are to be found in two publications by R. Binns: *From Speech to Writing*, Scottish Curriculum Development Service, Edinburgh, 1978 and 'A technique for developing written language' in M. M. Clark and T.

Glynn, *Reading and Writing for the Child with Difficulties*, Birmingham University, 1980

28   A. F. Scott, *The Poet's Craft*, Cambridge, Cambridge University Press, 1957; Wallace Hildick, *Word for Word*, London, Faber & Faber, 1965; R. Skelton, *The Poet's Calling*, London, Heinemann, 1975.

29   William Sansom, *The Birth of a Story*, London, Chatto & Windus, 1972.

7

RECEIVING THE WRITING

The teacher's response

How teachers respond to children's written work depends on what they are looking for and what they see as the purpose of the operation. When Barnes asked teachers in eleven secondary schools what they saw as important in receiving pupils' written work, 76 per cent said correcting errors, 41 per cent assessment and only 21 per cent replying and commenting on the work.[1] The term 'marking' is still conventionally used to cover at least four quite separate operations, which teachers frequently try to carry on simultaneously:

a) Responding to the writing as an interested reader, commenting on it, discussing its effect, raising questions.

b) Assessing the work by some explicit or instinctive set of standards or comparisons, grading or awarding a mark (see pages 187–95).

c) Correcting errors or proof-reading (see pages 195–204).

d) Monitoring the work for two separate evaluative purposes:

    i) to diagnose the particular needs of the individual pupil;

    ii) as feedback about the relative success of the teaching and as prognosis for future work (see pages 211–17).

The first of these should be the dominant activity. Responding to pupils' writing really demands something of the openness that we bring to other kinds of text, a willingness to be moved or interested or excited, a making of meaning by bringing something of ourselves to the words on the page. In fact, of course, the marking context frequently militates against this. Not only is there the pressure of thirty books to mark, the very fact that as we read we begin to make corrections or marginal comments makes it harder for us to respond to the work as a whole. Indeed, some teachers guard against any involvement; they see the aim of what they are doing as essentially objective; to assess the work, sum it up, award it a mark, in a way that might be duplicated by any other teacher. They 'read' the work not as a potential experience but as the cue for their own activity; they are becoming machines for marking in senses (*b*) and (*c*) above. The primacy of sense (*a*) was summed up in one of the early Schools Council Bulletins:

> If the judgement upon a piece of writing is to do it justice the marker must respond to it in a more personal way, a way that reflects his outlook, his attitudes, his personality.[2]

An American teacher, Peter Elbow, has vividly described how he came to transform his approach to commenting on student papers, a task which used to make his head swim. He originally had clear ideas of what he was looking for, but somehow the premises and the practice didn't hold together.

> The more I thought about it, the more it seemed that these professional, objective matters of diction, organization, and argument *weren't what determined how I responded to the paper.*

> But if I tried to say *how* and *why* I actually did respond, I was immediately out of bounds: it was all mixed up with my mood and my personal quirks or taste and my temperament.[3]

Instead of trying to be fair and objective, he set about the equally difficult task of being openly subjective:

> actually trying to give a full and accurate report of what went on in me as a result of reading the words on the paper: no matter how little I understood why I was having these thoughts and feelings and even if they seemed nutty.
>
> No doubt I often missed the real truth about my reactions. But the new struggle seemed better. I felt it made the whole transaction between writer and reader much more genuine. I felt it helped the student's writing a bit more. It was much more fun. And it seemed to increase my powers of perception: simply to start writing a comment of this sort often led me to notice something about the paper that was very interesting – and helpful to the student – but something I never would have noticed if I had stuck with trying to be fair, professional, and objective.[4]

The contrasts between comments which are intended by the teacher to be 'objective' and impersonal and those which deliberately stress a personal response are neatly illustrated in *Mark My Words*. In that book, the whole of one boy's written output in school is examined. During his first year, all his writing in English was received with comments like 'Paragraphs!' or 'All one sentence, and not even a full stop at the end!' or 'Your writing is deteriorating. You are running your words together.' In the third year, such magisterial comments and commands were replaced by personal responses (not always favourable) to what the boy had written:

> Incredibly complex and original suggestions. Good thinking though I doubt if it would work in practice. What

happens when the plane arrives at the airport to find it blocked by snow or fog?

I like your description of this 'battle', it makes it sound like the real thing.

So what! Your ideas aren't bad but you have not put them over very clearly.[5]

At 14, students are clearly aware that there is a subjective element in marking, acknowledged or not. 'The comments on work are written depending on what sort of mood the teachers are in', says a girl, and a boy suggests that 'marking from one teacher for a whole term is misleading; there are some people who like some sorts of work and others who do not'. Their remarks make clear how much they value the feeling of personal contact, the sense of writing and marking as initiating a kind of dialogue with the teacher. As Tony Dunsbee has said, for many of them this may well be the *only* regular means of communication between teacher and taught. By comparison, grading and correcting seem of minor importance. Hull pupils' reactions to this process echo, not surprisingly, those previously reported in London, Coventry and elsewhere. They dislike too many red ink corrections and numerical marks or ticks instead of comments.

I think teachers should not sprawl red ink pen all over your work so as to spoil it and then they go and put it on the wall and it does not look very good at all.

I prefer teachers to read thoroughly the work but not always mark in red every mistake.

I think all work should be marked in pencil not red ink as this spoils it.

The marks in the margin do not mean a lot to me.

Putting just a tick on your work makes you think it wasn't worth it and that the teacher hasn't really read or looked properly at the work.

> I don't think when the teachers give a mark is very helpful. I would rather them just mark the spelling, grammar and vocabulary and not give a mark like 8 or 9.

Positively, what these pupils said they liked and found helpful were the teacher's comments ('a bit longer than either good or bad', said one) and any sense of individual contact and guidance.

> I like the teachers to write a comment which explains what you're doing wrong or right, or what needs improving; if they don't, you never know or learn.

> It's important to put a comment at the bottom of the writing explaining if it was amusing, detailed, etc, and if any improvements could be made.

> It is always good to have criticism so you know where to correct and improve your work next time.

Comments are helpful, then, but a number of pupils said that interaction was better:

> I prefer teachers to go through the writing with me so I can see the mistakes and I am able to correct them.

> I would prefer teachers to consult me on my own opinions on my work before and after marking, give me reasons for their marks and help me individually with my problems.

Research and experience confirm that the ways in which teachers respond to children's work, both in talk and in written comments, significantly affect their students' motivation, attitudes, way of working and rate of development. One experiment found that children who were given individualized comments scored better in their subsequent work than those who were given a stock comment or simply a grade.[6] Consider, then, the reactions of a boy in his first term at a new school whose opening piece of work was returned with no response to the content or suggestions but the simple comment 'Work *harder*. This is not enough'. The next six pieces of work were returned with no comments of any kind, simply a tick or a mark out of ten. The next four, in quick succession, were greeted by:

Work neatly and be more careful.

Be careful.

This is still careless.

This is *not* neat enough.

The climax was '$\frac{0}{10}$ I do not think you try'. We may not be surprised if by this time the boy was not trying. No interest had been expressed in him or his work. The teacher apparently imagined that issuing vague injunctions like 'work harder', 'work neatly', 'be careful', with no indication of *how* these changes were to be brought about, would produce automatic improvement. In fact, the effect of such a critical response is likely to be simply inhibiting. What the boy learns is that 'writing can damage your health'. By contrast, what are the basic principles for establishing what is sometimes called 'a climate of trust'?

a) Be personal. 'I liked this, John', is a more encouraging response to the first piece of work than simply 'Good'.

b) Concentrate on the major purpose of the writing. If it is a story, for example, respond positively to the effects it produces: how it builds up suspense, or makes you laugh, or interests you in the central character.

c) By asking questions, try to get the writer to view his or her own work critically: Would you talk to your father like this? Why was she so angry? What would the room have looked like?

d) Reinforce the good by calling attention to effective words, phrases or sections (Yes, that really does sound horrible! or, I like the conversation between the two girls) or by sharing your own experiences (I used to get into trouble like this too; perhaps we all feel like this at times).

e) Make practical suggestions about possible ways of improving the work rather than saying negatively what was
wrong with it. (Wouldn't it be more interesting if you
reported the actual words they said? Perhaps it would be
better to start with this section – what do you think?)

With encouragement of the kind suggested above children
are more likely to write their own thoughts and feelings,
rather than strive to produce artificially what they think the
teacher wants. They are also more likely to be prepared to
experiment, to take risks, which is essential for growth in
writing, if they feel secure about the teacher's interest and
support.

The process can be aided if pupils are encouraged to see
writing about their work as a dialogue, rather than as a one-
way commentary from the teacher, or if they keep informal
'journals' in which they can 'talk' informally on paper to the
teacher without any expectations of formal marking.[7] Some
find it easier to establish personal contact and to exchange
feelings in this way than to talk about their work.

When John, a less able boy, produced a half page of
observed detail about the pond where he fished, the teacher
wrote, 'I enjoyed this. I wonder how many fish you've caught
there since.' John replied underneath, 'Quite a few. We also
think there's a pike there.' He enjoyed the role of expert, and
was cheerfully scornful of the teacher's lack of practical
ability. When he explained how to make a bird box and the
teacher commented 'Well done John. You wrote this so
clearly that you made it seem simple', John responded briefly,
'It is.'

It has to be said that most English teachers are desperately
overworked by the marking burden, but also that some of the
time which they spend is wasted. The purpose of the exercise
is to ensure that the next pieces of writing are better than the
one under review. To keep writing 'Be more careful' on
successive pieces, or to note that the same errors are being

repeated weekly, ought to suggest that a new strategy needs to be tried. In fact, the *act* of marking as such has little of the mystic value that is sometimes attached to it. (It is significant that schools' comments on graduate students almost always pick out for special praise or blame that their marking is or is not up to date and thorough.) Most English teachers need to give more time to responding to their pupils' work and less to marking it. It was suggested in the last chapter that one major disadvantage of setting up the teacher as sole arbiter and editor of children's work was that it discouraged students from looking critically at their own writing and rehandling it. If the proposals made there for encouraging rewriting, and for working with students during the process, are practised, then there should be fewer occasions when all the books arrive at once for marking. However the programme is organized in a school, teachers should certainly consider reducing the burden and introducing more variety by following some of these strategies:

1 Marking selectively:
   a) Reading some pieces for total effect only, without any proof correcting and commenting fully on response to the work.
   b) Announcing beforehand that you will be concentrating on certain aspects of the writing, or certain classes of error, and ignoring others. (In my experience this does not lead as some sceptics claim to floods of other mistakes. Children do not normally make a deliberate attempt to be wrong.)
   c) Specifying the criteria by which this particular piece of writing will be judged, and concentrating marking upon those (e.g. establishing a particular mood, bringing the story to an effective climax, presenting an interesting conversation).
   d) Only marking the first few lines in detail, and reading the rest for general impression.

e) Planning groups of pupils, who will in turn have their work (i) marked in detail; (ii) commented on in writing; (iii) discussed with the teacher.

f) Larger-scale written projects, in which more can be achieved by discussion with individuals and less by collecting the work for detailed marking.

2 Shifting attention away from the teacher's marking:

a) Self-assessment. Pupils are encouraged to read and respond to their own work and to evaluate it by posing particular questions (see pages 215–16).

b) 'Contracting'. A version of self-assessment for older students, by which they specify beforehand what the writing is intended to achieve and what means are to be employed, and after completion assess how far the 'contract' has been met.

c) Pair or peer group assessment. A similar process to self-evaluation, but encouraging pupils to comment in a structured, constructive way about each other's work (see pages 216–17).

d) Round-robin assessment. Pupils in groups of four or five circulate their work with a blank sheet of paper attached, on which each writes comments and suggestions. After they have all read the three or four sets of remarks on their own work, they discuss the validity and helpfulness of these.

e) Providing a wider audience. Work can be displayed on the walls or read aloud (by the author or the teacher) as a preliminary to discussion (see pages 204–10).

The assessment of writing

We are carrying out an act of assessment every time we answer questions like: Is her work improving? How does John's story compare with Peter's? What grade does this deserve at 16+? Can we recommend her to train as a secretary? a teacher? Is he a good writer? All of these questions are essentially comparative, on a small or a large scale. They compare a piece of writing, that is, with what other students have done, or with what the individual has previously written, or with some abstract norm or an ideal model. That is why teachers who have to rank thirty or more pieces frequently divide them first into five groups, ranging from the best to the worst, and then subdivide within each of those groupings, comparing pieces with those closest to them. The judgements themselves will largely depend therefore on the expectations and experience of the markers. Research has shown that training increases the reliability of teachers 'scoring' children's writing.[8] Such judgements will depend heavily on what it is that the teachers are looking for. Studies show that assessment can be influenced by such apparently trivial details as children's first names, their sex and appearance, and the presentation of their work.[9] In two disturbing enquiries it was shown that handwriting had a major influence on examiners' marking.[10] When the same five essays were copied in different handwriting and presented to several English specialists, all five were awarded O-level pass marks when written in one style, but four out of five failed when written in another.

Some teachers and parents talk as though there is an agreed global concept called 'good writing' (like 'intelligence') which everybody can recognize. It's only too clear, though, that notions of good writing (and the criteria for recognizing it) vary from group to group, and for individuals within those groups. An employer's view of 'communicative competence' may not agree with the opinion of a professional writer judging a children's literary competition and seeking a lively individual voice, or with an O-level examiner or a scholar of linguistics. The first APU Primary report on *Language Performance in Schools* demonstrated convincingly that the apparent relative difficulty of four writing tasks changed dramatically according to the criteria by which the work was assessed.[11]

How can the comparative process of impression (or 'holistic') marking be made more effective and consistent? Because looking closely at and comparing examples of children's writing is crucial, probably the most useful guides for teachers have been the many scales published to assist in the assessment of relative merit in children's writing. In these, 'typical' examples of different levels of performance are ranked in order from the least to the most satisfactory. The order is normally based on the pooled judgements of a number of teachers or examiners. The most useful scales compare compositions on the same topic, or at least in the same mode (discursive essays, fictional narrative) and accompany them by comments drawing attention to the criteria by which the pieces are ranked as they are. Markers are encouraged to place a new piece along the scale, matching it with the one its features most resemble, and progressively by examining the range of writings and comments to 'internalize' the criteria. It is necessary to be aware, though, that teacher expectations change and that criteria shift. We can see this by comparing what have been two of the most influential scales put forward in this country.

In 1924, William Boyd was so sure of the ratings arrived at by his panel of markers that he claimed that they had an 'objective sureness', 'convincing proof that we have in the results the definite expression of a communal expert opinion which is the very essence of a standard of judgement'.[12] The outstanding essay by a girl of 11, judged almost universally by the panel to be excellent, was this one:

'A day at the seaside' – what pleasure is in those few words – for with them comes the echo of the waves lapping up on the golden sands, and the memory of those thrilling donkey rides!

To children who live in the smoky towns the experience of a visit to the blue sea is delightful, and one may well notice the eager looks on the faces, pinched and pale, of the slum children, as they are packed into the railway carriages, bound for the seaside.

The train ride, too, is a new experience, as one may see from their 'leaps' from window to window crying 'The sea!' 'The sea!'

Poor little mites, is it not sad to think that they have come into this beautiful world only to see the lovely country and seaside once in so long a while. However the train steams into a small station, where the happy youngsters alight, and after their teacher (for doubtless they are some little flock belonging to a Sabbath School) has seen that no one is lost, she points out the shimmering sea in the distance, and laughing with glee, they all march joyfully down the path, perhaps singing some glad refrain.

They at length reach the sands where myriads of gay children are dancing happily in the summer sunshine, and after throwing off their caps and coats they run away along the sands ready to join in their friend's play, or bathe in the cool delicious waters of the deep, blue sea.

Boyd's greatest praise for what he calls 'a highly exceptional production' is that the essay's merits 'suggest an adult rather than a juvenile mind'. The chief virtues are 'the elevated style and the detached point of view', the 'rich and varied' vocabulary ('the adjectives are particularly good'), the 'unusual number of rhetorical devices' and 'an adventurous use of punctuation'. There are only 'slight lapses' in spelling and punctuation.

What is omitted by Boyd is as interesting as what is included. There is no mention of such qualities as originality, closeness of observation, perceptiveness or sense of an individual voice (indeed, Boyd praises particularly the 'detached' point of view, remarking approvingly that the words 'I' and 'we' are never used in the essay). By comparison some of Boyd's comments on lower-rated essays are significant for their light on merits he clearly considered *less* important than those which elevated the outstanding one quoted. Graded below those pieces rated 'excellent' or 'decidedly above the average' came 'satisfactory' essays, about some of which Boyd wrote such comments as these:

a lively but rather undiscriminating imagination.

The description ... calls up a clear picture ... has a personal touch about it.

Of one 'only just satisfying requirements', Boyd wrote that 'there is a depth of personal feeling rare – perhaps happily – in children's composition'. In other words, what is personal, imaginative, emotionally-felt, lively, vividly realized is rated considerably lower than the detached, elevated, fluent and rhetorically varied.

It is impossible to estimate the washback effect of this, but clearly it must have been important. Teachers who studied Boyd's volume, with its apparently scientific claims (objective ... proof ... standard), and who knew that it was likely to be used by examiners in the process of selection, must inevitably have been influenced in their own views of what marked good writing, in the models they offered their pupils, and in the ways they tried to get them to write.

The contrast between these ratings and comments and those of a scale first published in 1965 is dramatic. The LATE pamphlet *Assessing Compositions* ranked 28 pieces by 15-year-olds in London secondary schools, marking them from E to A, and ending with two pieces described as 'exceptional'. This is part of one of these, William's lengthy impression of 'The grief of an old woman'.[13] Written in the first person it describes how he is watching an exciting programme set in the American Civil War on the television one evening, while his grandmother knits. The telephone rings and his father comes in with the news that the boy's uncle Ed has died.

The knitting stopped. I wanted to laugh and call at Daddy

to get out of my way and let me watch the tele. I had to laugh. It was all one big joke. It had to be. Yes, any second now Daddy was going to burst out laughing. I turned my head and looked at my grandmother. She was no longer knitting or moving but staring straight at Daddy's face. Suddenly she said slowly and carefully, 'Oh my God' and dropped the knitting from her hands. Quickly and urgently now, 'My child, my child. What's she going to do? Oh my child Shirl, what's she going to do?'

Why did that wretched man have to go and die now? I want to watch the war programme. All of a sudden I felt very, very ashamed, ashamed that I wanted to watch a film of killing and death when my uncle, a living, talking human being had ceased. I was very ashamed yet I knew that I did want to watch the film.

After considering how they have all learned how to play their roles from watching TV, the episode ends like this:

I turned away from the door as Nanny, helped by Philip, swayed drunkenly out of the lounge into the dim lit hall. I picked up her coat and walked over to where she now stood at the far end. I had not noticed before but her stockings were rolled down and lay in loose, untidy folds on her ankles. She looked like some female tramp, her short white-grey hair untidy, her strangely shaped ankles, her tearful worn face and her rough hands fallen at her sides. She stood like a puppet, swaying, allowing but not helping us to put her coat on for her. And all the time she spoke to someone about her girl. The policeman watched from the doorway. The cold night air came in. We guided her to the policeman, still speaking our lines. He took her and walked her slowly away, still talking, like some drunken criminal, into the cold yellow-black night.

Most readers would agree that this is exceptional for a fifteen-year-old but they would also feel that it was exceptional in a quite different way from the pieces that Boyd praised in those terms. The differences can be explained by the criteria which the LATE sub-committee formulated as the basis for their responses. Compare these with those mentioned earlier.

The first key question is 'Does the experience seem real?' Members of the group were concerned to ask how far the writing 'directly reflects the writer's own experience'; their judgements were in such terms as sincere, spontaneous and vivid. The second question is 'Has something been made of the experience so that it has significance for writer and reader?' The emphasis here is on imaginative coherence; less on pre-planning than on a sense of developing 'central direction'. The third key question is concerned with qualities of language: 'Is the language being used in a personally creative way, or does one word so determine the next that there are only clichés of thought, feeling and language?' Imaginative writing, says the Introduction, 'is concerned with what is unique'; realization depends on the use of 'significant detail'. Only lastly comes the question of mechanical accuracy, and this is significantly phrased. 'Is there adequate control of spelling and punctuation so that the child manages to communicate, and manages to do so without irritating the reader too much?' Instead of being a significant qualitative measure, accuracy is now presented as a low hurdle: adequacy is enough. (There are more than thirty mechanical errors in one of the pieces graded A.) Whereas Boyd thought he had produced a yardstick, 'a measuring device', the LATE group called their production 'a discussion pamphlet'.

To make the suggested comparison between Boyd's scale and the LATE one is not an artificial exercise in the history of education; it is of urgent practical importance. The apparent shift in the 1960s seems to be away from emphasis on qualities of language displayed for their own sake towards stress on the sincerity, the vividness, the truth to life with which experience is conveyed. The aim moved from adult models of impersonality towards the revelation of personal ideas and feelings appropriate to the age of the writer, from generally accepted truths and attitudes to unique perceptions. Rather than a stress on carefully planned form, in which insignificant content is decked out in imposing language, the emphasis was on the way in which the experience itself dictates the structure. Such changes had to involve accompanying changes in the role of the teacher, in methods of work, in the choice of reading, and in ways of responding to children's writing.

Has a revolution taken place? Well, yes and no. It is true that, given Boyd's 'outstanding' essays for comment, many teachers will now condemn them. They are seen as 'condescending', 'artificial', 'priggish', revealing 'unhealthy attitudes for a child', 'parroting adults', 'snobbish', 'overtaught', 'full of laboured clichés', 'totally lacking in real feeling' (to quote the comments of some teachers and students made to me). When W. H. Mittins gave three of Boyd's essays to readers of *The Use of English* for rating he found that many of his markers were torn between their admiration of the quoted author's 'enviable facility' and ability to absorb the language of books and their dislike of her 'implicit snobbery and derivative maturity', which made the piece 'nauseating in its second-hand unctuousness'.[14]

Nevertheless, now as in Mittins' enquiry, many teachers do grade essays more or less in the way that Boyd did, and rank their criteria similarly. Although the LATE pamphlet has been undeniably influential, marking experiments with teachers suggest that there is no widespread agreement with the grades allocated there. What seems to have been comparative unanimity about criteria in the 1920s and 1930s has disappeared. This breakdown of agreement can be illustrated by the reception of Schools Council Working Paper 9, *Standards in CSE and GCE*, 1967. Somewhat in Boyd's style, the authors provided what were described as 'secure touchstones': that is sections of essays together with examiners' comparative comments, explaining their reasons for the grades given them.[15] The insecurity of these touchstones became apparent, when Edward Blishen supported by a number of teachers said that he was 'furiously offended' by the assessment of the piece at the bottom of the scale which he described as 'a very revealing lapse of judgment'. He believed that as far as examiners were concerned, it showed that:

> what is plain, direct, relies on the force of simple language and is less than sophisticated in spelling and punctuation, is likely to be perceived quite unperceptively.[16]

Correcting errors

Here is a piece of writing that most English teachers will recognize as representative of the weaker work they regularly receive. A class of 13-year-olds have been engaged on a block of thematic work in which they were set to write about crowds from an assignment on a worksheet. This was Stuart's response:

The rugby crowd

When Hull FC got to the johplayer Special No 6 filal me and my friends was going. On the day I got up and get some sandwich. Then I went for my friends at 8.30 we we had to catch the trian we where off to Leeds.

On the train we had to give our tickets to the man as we was comeing to Leeds UTD fans thow soute at the train as we came in to the staion we found that all the fuzz was out they saw we was going on a rite in Leeds but the was everywhere we was walk along and a wines fan was off to the same match so we was wines fan but we had to buy a ticket to go into the match the crowd was shout and the game begain.

The temptation for a busy teacher, marking sequentially with red pen in hand, is simply to indicate errors as they occur and either to give up when enough red ink is on the book or to go on doggedly to mark over thirty mistakes. Proof-reading corrections of this kind become almost automatic; English teachers can hardly read letters from parents or friends without reaching for the red pen. Habits should be regularly questioned, though, and Stuart's description prompts queries that might be asked of most work that we mark.

1 What will be the probable effect of the red ink markings? We have seen that most students dislike such emphasis on mistakes, and they almost universally say that correcting errors is the least rewarding part of writing. Stuart has had his mistakes regularly pointed out for a number of years without very significantly affecting his work. To mark every error here will increase his sense of failure and will suggest that there is little point in trying to revise because there are too many different points needing attention. Worse, it may inhibit him from writing much the next time, if he fears that to do so will expose his inadequacy. We have to analyse the mistakes in order to decide which need to be called to Stuart's attention with some expectation that they may be eradicated. We are particularly concerned with those that prevent his meaning from being clear.

2 What are the significant shortcomings of the work? The important weaknesses are the failure to give any real sense of the crowd (which was the supposed topic) and the loose stringing together of events in the first person (singular or plural) in chronological order. As so often in this kind of writing, Stuart begins the narrative with getting up and stops just as he is reaching the real point of the writing. Such authors often find rewriting difficult or impossible because the writing is seen as an almost uncontrollable stream, which once started, cannot be stopped or altered. Dealing with surface errors must not prevent the teacher from trying to help Stuart to improve these crucial aspects of his work. It is not just that the style is bald but that there is a failure to realize either the characters mentioned (the

ticket collector, the police, the Widnes fan) or the author's feelings.

3 What classes of error might usefully be brought to the writer's attention? Intuitive diagnosis comes in here, prompting questions and possible answers. For example:

a) Why does Stuart begin with reasonably constructed sentences and then write his second paragraph without a single full stop? He handles sentences, including subordinate clauses, quite fluently but simply fails to separate them. Is he getting carried away or simply careless? Perhaps try reading aloud to demonstrate the effect. Possibly suggest 'If these were captions for pictures of the event, where would you change pictures, and therefore start a new caption?'

b) As Stuart spells correctly some fairly difficult words (special, friends, sandwich) what underlies the mistakes he makes? Some words seem to be spelled as said (wines for Widnes, rite for riot, perhaps soute), some are the result of confusion or interference from other words (where for were, comeing, possibly begain), and others look like carelessness (train is spelled correctly but also as trian, filal, thow for throw, staion). Perhaps select one category of error to mark, try to help Stuart to understand the principle underlying the mistakes and give practice in using the words correctly.

c) Why does Stuart seem to have so much trouble with some syntactical forms, and not with others? In almost all cases it seems to be because he transcribes idiomatic spoken speech directly into writing (me and my friends, I got up and get). In particular, there is the frequently repeated use of *was* for *were*:

   me and my friends was going

   as we was coming to Leeds

   they was everywhere

In fact *were* is never used, and it would be interesting to look at Stuart's previous work to see whether he has ever employed it in writing. A closer look shows how dependent he is on just a few verbal forms. Another repeated one is:

we had to catch
we had to give our tickets
we had to buy a ticket

It may be necessary to work on the difference between spoken and written forms, or to encourage more variety. One of the reasons for the verbal monotony, of course, is that almost all the sentences have *I* or *we* as subject. Stuart is perhaps not yet ready to re-handle the scene from the view of the police, say, but it would be helpful to see how he tackles assignments other than personal anecdotes.

Let us move now from the specific example of Stuart's piece to the general issues which it raises. In schools we seem to lay too much stress on surface errors (which are easily markable) and spend too much time trying to eliminate them by inappropriate methods. Such errors created a real barrier to intelligibility in only 50 scripts out of 3800 examined in the first APU Secondary Language survey. The real shortcomings were not of the kind that are simply marked by red ink:

Weak writing produced by 15 year olds was more likely to be found inadequate in terms of content and style than in relation to grammatical or orthographic conventions.[17]

Indeed, it may be suggested that the nature of their training encourages English teachers in particular to exaggerate the seriousness of error. They always seem to be looking for what is wrong, rather than for what is right. This is partly because they themselves feel under pressure. Employers write indignantly to the papers complaining of children who split infinitives or misspell as though these were moral lapses. Young teachers say, 'If I don't mark every mistake, then the parents complain.' One head teacher told an assistant that she had not marked a set of books, because she had only written lengthy comments at the bottom of each piece. If we give the impression, though, that identifying all mistakes is exclusively the *teacher's* job, then we can hardly be surprised if children are happy to leave us to do it, rather than trying to look for their own errors.

What of eliminating these mistakes? The assumption that textbook exercises will produce a marked increase in accuracy is not supported by evidence. The Burrus study in the USA found that over three years pupils in groups engaged in 'real communication' were significantly superior in spelling and punctuation to those in groups that had been using exercises designed specifically to improve language accuracy.[18] George Sampson pointed out long ago that the correcting ritual when work is returned was generally 'a hideous sacrifice of time and effort. The only compositions that can be corrected are those that least need correction'.[19] Many of us have discovered that out-of-context spelling tests seem to help precisely those children who would learn the correct spellings anyway from their reading and do little or nothing to help the less able.

Whatever the sometimes unfair demands made on them, English teachers have to accept the responsibility of deciding on a rational marking and remedial policy in the interests of their children and in the light of available research. Writing like Stuart's prompts such conclusions as these:

1 We need to pitch our corrections at the level of the individual. Perhaps because our judgements of writing tend to be by some absolute standard, we may see all deviations from 'correct' English as faults to be eliminated at once, rather than distinguishing between those that are and those that are not significant at the writer's stage of development. We have to learn to diagnose what errors can and should be corrected by an individual at this particular time and to decide how to approach the problem in a way that will increase the chances of learning. Sometimes, when the

efforts are proving too time consuming for the teacher or too demanding for the pupil, they may simply have to decide to cut their losses and leave the problem.

2 We need a clearer order of priorities. Some weaknesses are more serious than others because they impair the quality of the writing more, they are global in their effects rather than superficial features of a single word. Such a discriminating hierarchy might be:

a) Weaknesses of the whole piece of writing, e.g.:
   structure, coherence and sequence, relevance, effectiveness, focus.

b) Weaknesses of paragraphs and sentences, e.g.:
   development, appropriate connections, lack of sentence variety, awkward or confused sentences, inability to write in sentences.

c) Weaknesses in relating words to each other, e.g.:
   subject-verb agreement, consistency of tenses, framing of phrases and clauses, case of pronouns.

d) Weaknesses in mechanics, e.g.:
   spelling, punctuation, use of capitals and abbreviations.

e) Weaknesses of language variation, e.g.:
   inappropriate register, questionable use of slang or dialect.

In terms of successful writing, the first two of these five categories are most important, but the bulk of teacher corrections concentrate on the last three.

3 We should make explicit what we think we are doing. Pupils, their parents and others deserve to know what our policy is over correcting work, and increasing numbers of schools send a statement to all homes. Children are often confused because teachers not only seem to have different aims in marking but also use different symbols for indicating errors. Tony Dunsbee found in a single school sixteen different ways of indicating a spelling mistake and ten ways of showing ambiguity of meaning.[20] A Department should

be able to agree on tactics. The early meetings with a new class are often a good time to make the functions of marking more explicit, and to involve the pupils in considering what kinds of help are appropriate.

We need to make criticism and correction more of a shared activity and less a solitary one. After discussing their feelings about corrections and comments, it is helpful to make children become markers themselves. They can be given three or four pieces on the same topic to rank in order of merit, and then be asked to compare and justify their decisions. They can be given a piece from another class on which to write comments, and then the comments themselves can be examined and discussed in terms of their accuracy and helpfulness to the writer. Such introductory activities can lead to work on writing they themselves have done. Distribute unmarked work so that everybody has someone else's (or possibly photocopy half-a-dozen pieces, so that several pupils have the same). Ask them to mark these as helpfully as possible, remembering the points made in discussion. Then return the work to the original writers, and ask them to jot down their reactions to the marking (or, in the other case, form groups to compare different reactions to the same piece). Finally reconsider, in the light of this experience, what the chief problems of marking are and what kinds of help children think that marking can provide.

4 Errors should be seen as a necessary, even desirable, feature of learning. We all develop our language capability by a process of trial and error. The child who never uses a word she cannot spell and writes throughout in simple sentences may not make mistakes, but will also not make much progress. Like miscue analysis in reading, errors are valuable signals to the teacher about the stage of development which the child has reached and about the kind of learning that is required for further progress.

5 Many errors are rooted in the fact that young or less able

children are unfamiliar with the way in which writers behave. They have been speaking confidently and using the essential structures of the language for years, but they know a great deal more than they can actually demonstrate in writing, a form with which they are much less familiar. The boy who wrote of a book, 'I didn't reckon nothing to it he must of been stupid writing it' transcribed as regularly as he could what he would have said to a friend. Children who work very slowly drift from one construction to another in mid-sentence, because their attention is fixed on a limited span; each part is correct, but the whole construction is not. So a girl of 11 writes of a picture of a tramp:

> His trousers they were mucky and his hands wer not very clean ... I could not help to look at him.

In this respect, shifting from talking to writing is for some students not unlike the process of learning a foreign language: the learner passes through an intermediate stage (which Selinker has called Interlanguage)[21] in which systematic errors occur. The writer is striving to produce sentences in the 'new' language but without being able to use naturally the forms of native speakers of that language (i.e. mature writers). A number of Selinker's ideas, like transfer-of-training (the overgeneralization of a rule that has been taught), can be applied usefully to learning to write. When children are taught the apostrophe to indicate possession, some of them will then put the apostrophe before every plural s. They may even do exercises in the apostrophe quite correctly only to lapse again when engaged on free writing. The evidence is, though, that many syntactic problems simply disappear as a result of more writing.

It is impossible to deal adequately here with classroom methods for increasing accuracy in writing, but a few principles can be proposed. When working with a group:

1 Remember the evidence, summed up by Andrew Wilkinson,[22] that the direct teaching of grammatical structures has no beneficial effect on pupils' writing. If you wish to teach a syntactical error or ambiguity, or to introduce a grammatical term, work *from* examples *towards* the concept, and give models on which the pupils can base their own writing. Collect examples where possible from the pupils' own work, and use these as the basis for discussion and rewriting.

2 Encourage successive drafting, in which 'corrections' are seen as a stage in a process, rather than as a terminal judgement. Sometimes limit the amount written. Try sentence-combining and transformation exercises, particularly those which draw materials from the pupils' own work. Encourage group response and group revision.

3 Teach similar language forms together, not confused forms. To teach ITS and IT'S, THEIR and THERE may seem to produce immediate results, but the long-term effect is often to *increase* confusion. Teach IT'S with THAT'S, WHAT'S; ITS and THEIR with other possessive forms THERE with WHERE and HERE, etc.

4 In punctuation, try to concentrate on correct punctuating of pupils' *own* work. If you want the class to add punctuation marks to unpunctuated prose, use *spoken* language as the basis (since this genuinely has no punctuation until they write it down) rather than the artificial exercise of written prose without stops. Generally, however, accuracy has to be pursued individually or in small groups. This depends on –

   i) accurate diagnosis, by close observation of pupils' talking, reading and writing and error analysis;

   ii) the keeping of records – either your own notes, or using the school's check list of writing abilities;

   iii) devising specific help for individuals, or for small groups shown by your diagnosis to have the same particular need. For example:

5 Encourage pupils to observe themselves, as spellers, and to seek for reasons for misspelling (slips of the pen, confusions, phonetic spelling, idiosyncrasies of the English spelling system). Ensure that dictionaries are available and used. Encourage students to keep their *own* lists of correct spellings of words they misspelt. Give regular time for them to test each other. Introduce the sequence 'look–cover– spell aloud–write–check' as a learning device. Perhaps start to work on those misspellings that can be covered by the application of simple rules.

6 Assist individualized learning by providing some of the simple learning programmes on cards or in books that deal with specific points of punctuation or syntax to which children can be referred. It is sometimes better if they can work in pairs on these.

7 Shift the focus, by asking a student to read work on to tape or by having it typed or projected on a screen, to produce a new perspective, and then asking what changes or corrections now seem necessary.

8 Try to organize the pattern of work so that there are regular periods of time in which most pupils are busy on their own or in groups, and when you can give essential individual tuition. Record what you do with each individual or it is quickly forgotten. Try not simply to explain, but to give each pupil something specific to do in order to 'fix' the learning. Tackle *one* thing at a time, especially with weaker pupils.

Sharing and publication

Writing should not automatically end up in what James Moffett has called 'the dead-letter office of a teacher's desk'.[23] The feeling that nobody will take any notice of what you have written must be one of the major reasons that people do not write. Many teachers have found that providing a real audience for pupil-writing has been one of the most important ways of improving attitudes towards writing, and thus the writing itself. This is not to say that all work done in school should be shared. Some children will be writing essentially for themselves, their work is private, confessional, tentative or experimental. It may be shared with a sympathetic teacher, but it is not for general consumption.

When pupils of the 'sensitive' ages 13–14 were asked how they felt about other people reading their work, only a small minority said that they definitely disliked it. Those who felt this way explained their feelings like this:

I hate people looking at my work, people like mum and dad, because they always find mistakes and they think it should be perfect.

people tend to pick at pieces of it and can sometimes make me angry when they call out, 'Oh look at this, he's put...'.

Sometimes I feel ashamed about my work ... and I don't like other kids reading it, because I get embarrassed.

I dislike friends or parents reading my work because they, like teachers, have to complain about something or other, or usually just laugh at it.

The impression is given that these children have been affected by insensitive, fault-finding reception of their work. Fortunately they are outnumbered by those who like having their work read by others. A girl of 14 says, 'I think it is important because otherwise what is the point of writing it unless it is just for self-enjoyment.'

The commonest response is the understandable one, 'It all depends ...'. Whether or not students of this age enjoy seeing their work made available to a wider audience depends on whether or not they themselves are satisfied with it, on the attitudes of the readers, and on the way in which the work is presented. As one 14-year-old said,

I don't like other people reading my work if it is bad, but if it's good, I don't mind. It also depends on who is reading it.

> Some people I really hate reading my work, but other people I don't mind.

This is a simple expression of the distinctions: good work/bad work, friendly/unfriendly readers. Something of the range of insights can be conveyed by brief examples from the replies of other pupils of 13 and 14:

> I don't mind people reading my work because I like reading theirs. I don't like them reading it if they say something like 'Mine's better' because they would be hurt if I said it to them and to me that is not caring how others feel.

> If people read my work I go all shy, I prefer them to read it when I'm not there.

> I don't mind friends reading and correcting my work but I hate having to stand up and read my work aloud.

> I like people to give an honest opinion and I also enjoy reading other peoples then you can see if yours is as good or needs a little more thought.

> When people read your work they tend to compare it with other people's work. This is wrong most of the time.

It is clear from comments like these that a great deal depends on the way in which the teacher sets up the sharing of work, the creation of a supportive audience that will give a sympathetic response to writing and make positive suggestions about it. Writing is for sharing. However, when Barnes investigated the practice of teachers in eleven secondary schools, he found that only a quarter of them 'published' children's writing in any way.[24]

It may be helpful to distinguish between written assignments that are set up with a particular audience and purpose built in, and writing that is done for the teacher but then opened to a wider audience. In the first category come tasks like writing a letter to a member of the class who is in hospital, composing a story to be read to younger children in the school or preparing a booklet to introduce the school to newcomers. In the second category come such publishing ideas as small magazines, pages in the local paper or tie-ups with local radio. It doesn't really matter that most of these efforts are short lived; variety is probably more important than endurance.

Here is one example of the way in which an actual but unknown audience can be used as an incentive for varied writing styles and purposes. The English staff at a large city school and at a smaller rural comprehensive some miles away agreed that their first years should prepare 'dossiers' about their own schools for each other. A great deal of lively writing, illustrated by drawings and photographs, was produced. These were the original suggestions for children in one of the schools:

TELLING THE FIRST YEAR AT HOWDEN SCHOOL ABOUT WOLFRETON

Use as many illustrations as you can.

1 *Helping them to imagine what our school is like*

To help people imagine places you have to describe them – what you can see, and hear, and feel, and smell – what's happening there – how people are moving, talking, acting.

Here are some places and events you might describe – House assembly; tutor period; changing rooms; the gym; some lessons; bike sheds; practices for teams, orchestra, junior play; the bookshop; the dining hall; cycling to school; 3.50; science lab; favourite spots; the head's office; staircase between lessons; art room ... and others?

Or choose *two* and write longer descriptions, more like stories.

continued overleaf

---

2 'My *own* experiences'

Write the story of *one* of the things that's happened to you this year at school. Remember that first years at Howden won't know people at Wolfreton.

Some ideas for your story – the first day; getting into trouble; the best match/performance/trip/lesson; a fight; the day everything went wrong; meeting?; the best day this year ... any others?

Make your story entertaining to read.

3 *Explaining things*

People will understand Wolfreton better if you can explain things to them. Choose *one or two* from this list.

    Draw a plan of the school buildings *and* explain the things that are important. Discuss this with someone.

ii) Compare this school with your last school. Make a list of the things you'll compare before you start.

iii) If you've seen a lot of Grange Hill programmes, and/or read the books, compare this school with Grange Hill. Make a list first of the things you'll compare.

iv) If you know someone well who's at the Upper School, interview him/her about the differences between the two schools. Then write a report of your interview.

v) Think about the subjects you've done this year and about the lessons. What interesting things have you learnt? What makes good and bad lessons? Then, write about what you've learnt this year and about how you've learnt it.

4 *Things about Wolfreton that teachers wouldn't dream of*

What are they? Write about some of them in any way you choose. Some suggestions of ways to write – lists; rhymes; diary entries; letters; short plays; poems; explanations to go with photographs; interviews written up; advertisements; newspaper articles.

Some of the possible ways in which children's writing has been shared more widely can be briefly listed:

Readings:	live readings by pupils to a group,
	    the whole class,
	    another class,
	    writing workshop or literary group;
	recorded readings on audiotape for
	    the class collection,
	    departmental use elsewhere as
	      a resource,
	    broadcasting on local radio;
	recording on videotape.

Single text
for others
to read:
	preserved in
	    class collection,
	    departmental or library stock;
	available outside school for
	    parents,
	    friends,
	    governors;
	exchange with others –
	    individual exchanges and 'twinning'
	      with people in other classes,
	    group exchanges between
	      secondary schools,
	    group exchanges between
	      secondary school and feeder
	      primary school.

Display:	single texts within the school, in the
	    classroom,
	    corridors or hall,
	    library;
	in the community, in the
	    library,
	    shops,
	    municipal offices,

art galleries and museums;
groups of texts:
the work of one class in another's
classroom,
illustrated thematic group of work,
poster poems,
wall magazines.

Publish multiple
copies:
duplicated or printed
magazine of work,
anthology;
entries in school magazine or newspaper;
school column or page in local newspaper.

Publishing in any of these ways takes time and effort, but it can be rewarding. One school claims to sell 4000 copies of a creative writing periodical printed in offset-litho. A videotape of children of different ages reading their own work has aroused interest and a desire to write in several of a city's schools. The annual *Daily Mirror* literary competition and the contest for the best school magazines are not only important for the winners but for the encouragement of seeing what others of the same age can do.

Evaluation

Ultimately teachers have to ask how far the goals they set for their writing programmes are being achieved. It should be axiomatic that:

a) teachers do their own evaluating (you cannot adequately 'inspect' the achievement of other people's goals);

b) the evaluation arises from the actual work done (not from additional special tests which destroy interest in writing and distort what is supposed to be measured);

c) the purpose of evaluation is to promote learning (unlike testing, it looks back only to look forward).

We are, of course, also concerned with the interlocking issue of how our *students* are evaluating the programme they are following. I have found it helpful at the end of terms to encourage them to write 'reports' on their work in English and to discuss which activities seem to have been most productive, and why. Some examples of comments of this kind have appeared at intervals throughout this book. For evaluating the progress made by a group in writing, and the relative success of the teacher's strategies, there are therefore three main sources of insight: continuing observation of the writing process, occasional analysis of the work done over a period, and the students' own evaluation of themselves and their work.

CONTINUING OBSERVATION

There are real problems in trying to evaluate the success of teaching strategies and the evidence of learning in a non-linear subject with such varied goals and such an overlap with other subjects. The important thing is to refine the instinctive blanket judgements which we all make when working with a class.

For convenience we can divide these observations roughly into those considering the group in general and those which are of individuals. Looking at the class as a whole, engaged in writing, we are asking such questions as:

a) How does their response to this assignment compare with their reaction to others? Were there marked differences between individuals' responses?
b) What were their reactions to the pre-writing activities – reading, talking, stimulus? To what extent did these lead effectively into writing? How far did pupils seem to want to write?
c) Were they keener to talk than to write? How difficult did it seem for them to begin writing, and how long did it take?

d) What sorts of help are being requested? Who prefer to write alone undisturbed? Who feel a continuing need to share with others?

e) Do students' comments and suggestions show developing understanding of the writing process? In what ways do they respond to and propose changes in each other's ideas?

f) What kinds of planning are in evidence? What attitudes are shown towards revision? How much rereading and revising goes on?

g) What varieties of working pattern are observable? How much time is being spent in actual writing?

Our consideration of individuals will draw particularly on our conferences with them about their writing, and on any dialogues in written form. We may wish to make this essential personal contact more systematic by examining the work for particular features and logging these, or entering details on a check-list. Essentially we are concerned with what achievements mark the individual's work, what limitations and constraints are imposed on it, and what immediate development we might wish to aim at. We are therefore examining such features as these:

a) The range of modes and subjects on which the child writes. (Some individuals seem able to turn any assignment into the same subject or style.)

b) The range of audiences for whom writing is done.

c) Signs of stylistic development (e.g. moving from first person to consistent third person narrator, ability to present the actual words of dialogue, empathy with an imagined character).

d) The amount written on various topics. (How far does it appear to correlate with enjoyment and with fluency?)

e) The features of syntax or punctuation which are demonstrably understood (e.g. uses relative clauses after subject as well as after object, uses 'whom' correctly, tries to employ semicolon).

f) structural qualities (e.g. ability to start a story from within the chronological sequence, coherent paragraphing of essay, logical development of argument).

SYSTEMATIC CONSIDERATION OF DEVELOPMENT

These observations made as the work goes along may need to be reinforced periodically by assessing pupils' progress against existing models. It has already been suggested that such an assessment should be based on the actual work done, rather than on special tests, and that the results will depend on the criteria with which we approach the task. There is clearly no one ideal measure, but the most helpful guidance for classroom teachers at the moment seems to be in the work of Andrew Wilkinson, whose recent book ends:

> Our approach considers the question of how children develop as people – and thus the emotional, moral and cognitive education that is offered. In other words language is inseparable from living.[25]

The emphasis on development, and on the inseparability of writing development and personal development, offers us a conceptual frame within which we can 'place' children's writing from four standpoints: cognitive, affective, moral and stylistic. The model attempts to draw together the work of experts in language (like Moffett and Britton), in moral development (like Kolberg) and in other fields, to provide a hierarchical structure that might serve us as a means of assessing our students' progress.

As one example, drawn from the affective part of the model, Wilkinson and his Crediton Project team suggest that distinct stages of development can be construed from the way in which the writer expresses a sense of the self, of others, of the reader, of the environment and of reality. The successive stages of awareness of other people, for instance, are detailed as:

1 recording the mere existence of other people as having been present;
2 indicating the separateness of others by, e.g. giving their words or significant actions;
3 presenting the thoughts and feelings of others by quoting their actual words or describing them, or actions indicating them;
4 making analytical, interpretive comments on aspects of character and behaviour;
5 giving a consistently realized presentation of another person by a variety of means;
6 revealing ability to see person and interactions in extended context.[26]

Similar sequences are suggested for each of the other areas mentioned. In these cases, it is the stage reached under each heading that leads eventually to the establishment of a kind of 'profile' for a piece of writing. The model is grounded in the writing of children of seven, ten and thirteen, and the different stages are exemplified by specific examples. Summarized in a twelve-page outline at the back of the book, it helps to refine teachers' awareness of the marks of increasing maturity in their own pupils' work, and to make comparisons between pupils more coherent. Other useful work, with a similar purpose, is being done by John Dixon, whose notion of 'staging points' in children's progress is being worked out both in relationship to middle school children (with the Bretton Hall Language Development Unit)[27] and to 16-year-old examination candidates (with Leslie Stratta).[28] With Irene Farmer, he has written, 'As teachers we say it is progress rather than performance in language that it's vital to assess.'[29]

STUDENTS' SELF-EVALUATION

There are, of course, other people whose perception of progress in writing may be helpful; the comments of parents and of other subject teachers may point to considerations which we have missed. A programme of self-evaluation by students is particularly important, however, not only because of the guidance it offers the teacher, but also because it is a strategy that helps the students themselves, especially from about 13 onwards.

In the early stages, self-evaluation needs to be prompted by specific questions, which need to be varied. They should not be asked of every piece of work, or of every student. The results can be discussed with the individuals, and occasionally with the class as a whole. Students who have engaged in this process can later be asked (in years four and five, say) to evaluate work without the need of specific questions. When first attempting this work, though, teachers have found that it helps to ask such things as:

How much time did you spend in writing this?

Where did you get your ideas for it?

What was the hardest thing about writing it?

When you read it over, what are you most satisfied with?

What do you see as the weaknesses of what you have written?

Were you trying to do anything new or to experiment in any way with this writing? If so, what were you trying to do, and how far do you feel you have succeeded?

Put a tick alongside any words, phrases or longer passages that you think are particularly good.

Put a question mark by any sections that you are not really happy about, or that you think might be revised or corrected.

What sort of help with your writing do you think would be most useful now?

If you could improve one aspect of your writing, what would it be?

What will you try to achieve in your next piece of writing?

Looking back over your work this year, what do you think has improved?

Which of the assignments for writing have you most enjoyed? Try to explain your reasons.

Which work done by other pupils have you most enjoyed hearing or reading? What was it about that work which you particularly enjoyed?

Classes which are used to sharing and to small group work may prefer to move from self-evaluation to peer-group evaluation. An elementary way of preparing for this is for pairs of children to read each other's work and then, without referring to the text, to tell back to the author what he or she seems to be saying, or to narrate the story as precisely as possible. The author can then point out significant alterations or omissions. This is one way of focusing attention on what is unclear or ineffective. From summarizing, pairs or small groups can go on to describing their experience as readers: saying what they understood, felt, imagined as they progressed through the text. In the early stages it may be sensible to ban judgements, especially negative ones. In the small scale, children who are considering each other's work can be asked to pick out the best sections (and to indicate why they are effective) or to select parts that need revising (and then the group can attempt to re-draft them).[30] In the large scale, they can be asked what responses as readers they have to the writing which suggest that it is effective, what specific things the writer might do to improve the work, or what goals they think the writer should now be aiming at. There is some research evidence from America that the improvement in writing ability when peer evaluation is used equals or may exceed that when the teacher carries out the evaluation procedure alone.[31]

References

1 Douglas Barnes and Denis Shemilt, 'Transmission and Interpretation', reprinted in Barrie Wade, *Language Perspectives*, London, Heinemann, 1982.

2 J. Britton, N. Martin and H. Rosen, *The Multiple Marking of English Composition*, London, HMSO, 1966, p. 10.

3 Peter Elbow, *Writing Without Teachers*, New York, OUP, 1973, p. 119.

4 ibid., pp. 119–20.

5 Tony Dunsbee and Terry Ford, *Mark My Words*, London, Ward Lock, 1980, pp. 20ff.

6 E. B. Page, 'Teacher comments and student performance', *The Journal of Educational Psychology*, August 1958, 49, No. 4, pp. 173ff.

7 See Jerre Paquette, 'The Daily Record', *The English Magazine*, Spring 1982, No. 9, pp. 34–6 and Kevin Eames, *Whatever Comes to Mind*, Cherwell Learning about Learning Booklet No. 3, County Hall, Wiltshire.x

8 Some of this work is conveniently summarized in Charles R. Cooper and Lee Odell, *Evaluating Writing*, Urbana, Illinois, NCTE, 1977, pp. 18ff.

9 Evidence summarized in R. Wood and W. A. Napthali, 'Assessment in the classroom: what do teachers look for?', *Educational Studies*, October, 1975, 1, No. 3, pp. 151ff.

10 Dennis Briggs, 'The Handwriting Handicap', *Where*, June 1971, No. 58, pp. 170–3 and 'A study of the influence of handwriting upon grades using examination scripts', *Educational Review*, June 1980, 32, No. 2, pp. 185–93.

11 Assessment of Performance Unit, *Language Performance in Schools*, Primary Survey Report No. 1, London, HMSO, 1981, pp. 108–9.

12 William Boyd, *Measuring Devices in Composition*,

Spelling and Arithmetic, London, Harrap, 1924, pp. 36–7.

13 LATE, *Assessing Composition*, A discussion pamphlet, London, Blackie, 1965, pp. 40–2.

14 W. H. Mittins, 'Marking composition – a report', *The Use of English*, Winter 1960, 12, No. 2, pp. 88–92.

15 Schools Council Working Paper 9, *Standards in CSE and GCE: English and Mathematics*, London, HMSO, 1967, pp. 9–12.

16 *Where*, July 1974, No. 94, p. 207.

17 Assessment of Performance Unit, *Language Performance in Schools*, Secondary Survey Report No. 1, London, HMSO, 1982, p. 100.

18 D. J. Burrus, 'A three-year comparative study of the functional approach to teaching the mechanics of language', PhD dissertation, Oklahoma State University, 1970.

19 George Sampson, *English for the English*, Cambridge, Cambridge University Press (1921), 1952 ed, p. 64.

20 Dunsbee and Ford, op cit., pp. 46–7.

21 Larry Selinker, 'Interlanguage' in John Schumann and Nancy Stenson, *New Frontiers in Second Language Learning*, Newby House, USA, 1974.

22 Andrew Wilkinson, *The Foundations of Language*, Oxford, Oxford University Press, 1971, pp. 32–5.

23 James Moffett and Betty-Jane Wagner, *Student-centered Language Arts and Reading, K–13*, Boston, Mass., Houghton Mifflin, 1976, p. 150.

24 Barnes and Shemilt, op cit., p. 159.

25 Andrew Wilkinson *et al.*, *Assessing Language Development*, Oxford, Oxford University Press, 1980, p. 225.

26 ibid., p. 229.

27 Bretton Language Development Unit, *A Policy for Writers 9–12*, Bretton Hall College, 1981.

28 *Achievement in Writing at 16+*, Birmingham University (1981).

29 *The Times Educational Supplement*, 20 February 1981.
30 Examples of pupils discussing each other's work are given in Helen Savva and Bronwyn Mellor, 'Designing the Workshop', *The English Magazine*, Spring 1982, No. 9, pp. 27–30.
31 Mary H. Beaven, 'Goal setting and evaluation', in Charles R. Cooper and Lee Odell, *Evaluating Writing*, Urbana, Illinois, NCTE, 1977, p. 151.

PART 3:
REFERENCE SECTION

RESOURCES FOR WRITING: AN INTRODUCTORY CHECK-LIST

All experience is potentially a subject for writing, a 'resource' as that word is currently defined: 'anything which may be an object of study or stimulus for the pupil'. (Schools Council Working Paper 43, *School Resource Centres*). However, some materials specifically designed for classroom use to help in launching and developing classroom writing are obviously necessary. Most teachers find that their *own* resources – the pictures cut from colour supplements and mounted, the tapes recorded and edited in school, the booklets produced by a group of colleagues – are the most important ones. Because ideas frequently come from seeing what others have done, though, young teachers may find it helpful to examine critically the huge range of commercially produced materials some examples of which are listed here as likely to be in many departmental collections. Not all of these items are necessarily intended to help primarily with writing and not all of them will be suitable for any given group in school. The ability to choose and use resources is an essential professional skill.

Packs and kits

These are collections of different kinds normally including a number of the following: theme book, work cards, stencil-masters, slides or filmstrips, cassettes or records, posters or broadsheets, teachers' guide. Examples of titles are given when several are available within the series.

The Avon English Project, *(Cowboys and Indians My Desert Island City Life)* Bristol, Avon Resources

Cambridge Resources for English Teaching (*Stone, Wood, Metal, Plastic*; *Friends and Enemies*; *Extra-ordinary*) Cambridge.

The Childwall Project, *Design for Living*, London, Edward Arnold.

Craigie College Language Project, *Underground*, London, Holmes McDougall.

England A. W., *Caves* and *Islands*, London, Oliver & Boyd.

Lifescape series, pack 2, *Home, Neighbourhood and Community*, London, Architectural Press.

North West Regional Curriculum Development Project, *Situations*, London, Blackie.

People Around Us (Families, Friends, Work) ILEA with A. & C. Black.

Schools Council Integrated Studies packs *Exploration Man*, Oxford.

Schools Council & Nuffield Humanities Project Kits *(Education, War and Society, Relations between the sexes)* London, Heinemann.

Storypacks (Cokerheaton, Rushbrook), London, Evans.

You and Your Parents and others, London, Macmillan.

Thematic series

It is not difficult for teachers to build up their own collections of appropriate poetry and prose on a given theme, especially if they use such guides as Geoffrey Summerfield's *Topics in English*, Batsford, 1965, and T. E. Jeremiah's *A Source Book of Creative Themes*, Blackwell, 1972, or those two helpful subject indexes to poetry and prose, Helen Morris, *Where's that Poem?*, revised, Blackwell, 1974, and Colin and Susan Swatridge, *The Biblio File*, Blackwell, 1979. However, there are now many ready-made series of books or booklets on particular topics, frequently overlapping with each other, and examples of some of these are given below.

The Avon English Project ('Strange worlds', Autobiography', 'Witches and wizards'), Bristol, Avon Resources.

Checkpoints ('Advertising', 'Man and animals', 'The police') London, Edward Arnold.

Connexions ('His and hers', 'The language of prejudice', 'Food', 'Violence') Harmondsworth, Penguin.

Dimensions ('Love & marriage', 'Black & white', 'School') Oxford, Pergamon Press.

The English Project, stages 1, 2 and 3 ('Danger', 'Family & school', 'Ventures', 'Things working') London, Ward Lock.

Footprints ('Relationships', 'Work', 'Pleasure', 'Violence') London, Macmillan.

History at Source ('Children 1773–1890', 'Entertainments 1800–1900') London, Evans.

Investigations ('Change', 'The accident age', 'Shopping spree') London, Longman.

Schools Council General Studies Project ('Towns', 'Education', 'Living in Britain', 'Crime', 'Family') London, Longman.

Schools Council General Studies Project *Open English* ('Money', 'Sport', 'Food', 'Dreams') London, Longman.

Standpoints series ('All in the mind', 'Death', 'Change the street') Oxford.

Acland R., *Target English* ('Baby', 'Birds of prey', 'Flames')
Oxford, Blackwell.

Themes ('Encounters', 'Rebels'), London, Routledge & Kegan
Paul.

Jones, R., *Themes* ('Men & beasts', 'Conflict', 'Generations')
London, Heinemann.

Parker, T. H. and Teskey, F. J., *Themes to Express*, London,
Blackie.

Source and course books

A useful guide to the jungle of these publications is Pat Jones,
A Matter of Course, Wiltshire County Council, 1980. In
choosing such books, teachers need to consider questions
about the text's influence on the way in which writing is done
and judged, including these:

i) What is the audience? Is the book directly addressed to
the pupils? (If so, in what terms, and how realistically to
different abilities? is the book intended to be used by
children on their own?) Or is it meant for the teacher
(directly or indirectly? What rôle does it imply?) Or does
it shift from one to the other, or have no clear focus at all?

ii) What structure has the book? Is it to be followed through
or can the sections be used in any order? Is the arrangement thematic or in terms of skills learning or apparently
random? In what ways does it suggest that writing
abilities develop?

iii) What is the relationship to the teaching process? Does the
book itself try to teach directly? (giving information,
setting exercises, introducing passages?) Does it try to
suggest or to dictate what the teacher should do? What
balance of individual, small group and whole class work
is implied?

iv) How are different activities presented? Are possible
responses to extracts or pictures stipulated, suggested or
left open? Does the book say vaguely 'you could ...'? Are

suggestions or exercises intended for all pupils or some? Is there any grading of the work? Are the activities realistic in their assumptions? Can they be adequately monitored by the teacher? What resources do they demand?

v) What model of the writing process is presented, directly or by implication? What criteria of good writing are suggested?

Examples of other printed resources for writing

Copeman, C. and Self, D., *Poetrycards*, Basingstoke, Macmillan.
English Centre, ILEA, *Making a Newspaper,
Myself, Ourselves, The Unknown*
Great Newspapers reprinted, Peter Way.
Help the Aged, education pack.
Jackdaw folders (e.g. on Christmas, soccer, the Battle of Britain).
Mills, R., *Occasions* (with accompanying slides) London, Longman.

PICTORIAL

There is no substitute for one's own deliberately chosen collection of pictures, advertisements or cartoons without captions, but as examples of what is available:

Adland, D., *Visual Discussions* 1–3, London, Longman.
Argo posters (especially those without captions).
Bethell, A., *Eye-openers One and Two*, Cambridge, Cambridge University Press.
Gatter, M. and Kelly, N., *Photocards for English*, London, Edward Arnold.
Marland, M., *Pictures for Writing* and *More Pictures for Writing*, London, Blackie.
The Motor Car (large photographs and notes) Pictures and

Charts Ed. Trust.

Plimmer, F., *Impact* 1 and 2 (sets of thirty photo cards, with
   writing suggestions on reverse), London, Macmillan.
Progressive Picture Composition London, Longman (intended for T.E.F.L.).
Reading Pictures, London, BFI.

WORKCARDS

Abbs, P., *English Broadsheets*, Introductory set, first series,
   second series, London, Heinemann.
Copeman, C., *English Openings*, London, Ward Lock.
Foster, J., *Activity Factsheets*, London, Thomas Nelson.
Keys, J., *Take a Closer Look*, Aylesbury, Ginn.
Madeley, R. and Gibb, Sylvia, *The Writing Centre*, London,
   Blond Educational.
Taking Liberties A teaching pack for boys and girls on equal
   rights, London, Virago.

Audio-visual

This can be no more than a brief reminder of the sources from
which a large and growing range of material can be obtained.

i) BBC Schools radio programmes, especially series like
   Speak; Listening, Talking, Writing and the *Radiovision*
   programmes accompanied by slides. Contact Schools
   Broadcasting Department, BBC, Broadcasting House,
   London, W1A 1AA. The BBC also issues records, and
   their seven sound effects records are particularly useful.
   BBC Enterprises are at Villiers House, The Broadway,
   Ealing, London W5.

ii) BBC and ITV television programmes. Particularly useful
   for writing are series like ITV's *The English Programme*,
   Middle English and *Over to You* and the BBC's *Scene*.
   Although intended for younger children, *Picture Box*

often has helpful film material, and the teachers' notes include excellent thematic guides. Contact the education officer of your local ITV company, or the Education Secretary, Independent Television Companies Association, Knighton House, 52–66 Mortimer Street, London W1N 8AN.

iii) The British Film Institute's Education Department issues lists of short films, study extracts and slide sets appropriate for use in schools, together with a range of back-up materials for teachers. They are increasingly supplying stimulating packages like *Hammer: a cinema case study*. Contact the Education Department, BFI, 8, Dean Street, London W1V 6AA. The second edition of the *Video Source Book-UK* lists 5000 programmes.

A number of organizations issue film material intended for other school subjects that can be helpful for English (e.g. *History through the newsreels*, available from the Historical Association in conjunction with Macmillan).

iv) Gramophone records and cassettes. There is no single reference source. For English teaching the most useful publication is probably *The Gramophone Spoken Word and Miscellaneous Catalogue*, but this is only published at lengthy intervals. Reviews in monthly periodicals like *The Gramophone* may be helpful.

v) Slides. Probably the most comprehensive list is available from The Slide Centre, Portman House, Broderick Road, London SW17 7DZ.

vi) Other useful contacts:
The Society for Education in Film and Television (which issues the periodical *Screen*), 81 Dean Street, London W1V 6AA.
The National Audio Visual Aids Centre, 254–6 Belsize Road, London NW6.
The National Committee for Audio Visual Aids in Education, 33 Queen Anne Street, London W1M 0AL.

The Council for Educational Technology, 188 Great Portland Street, London W1.

Improvisations and simulations

Choosing the News, ILEA English Centre.

Jones, K., *Simulations: a handbook for teachers*, London, Kogan Page, 1980.

Lifeline, London, Longman (Schools Council Project in Moral Education).

Lynch, M., *It's Your Choice*, six role-playing exercises, London, Edward Arnold.

Nine Graded Simulations, ILEA (especially *Front Page* and *Radio Covingham*).

Pearce, J. *et al.*, *People in Touch*, London, Edward Arnold.

Schools Council General Studies Project, *Interplay*, London, Longman.

EXAMPLES OF CHILDREN'S WRITING

Many small, local collections of good children's work are available in printed or duplicated form, issued by NATE branches, local authorities, regional newspapers and even single schools. It is more difficult – outside the pages of David Holbrook and of works for teachers like those referred to here – to find examples of the writing done by average and less able children. Some general anthologies that are likely to be available in libraries are listed below.

Aston, A., *Poets in School*, London, Harrap, 1977.

Beckett, J., *The Keen Edge*, London, Blackie, 1965.

Children as Writers (winners of the *Daily Mirror*, now W. H. Smith, literary competition) London, Heinemann, annually.

Clegg, A.B., *Enjoying Writing*, London, Chatto & Windus, 1973.

Clegg, A.B., *The Excitement of Writing*, London, Chatto & Windus, 1964.

Ford, B., *Young Writers, Young Readers*, London, Hutchinson, 1965.

Hansen, I.V., *A Year's Turning*, London, Edward Arnold, 1970.

Holbrook, D., *Children's Writing: a Sampler for Student Teachers*, Cambridge, 1967.

ILEA English Centre, *City Lines*, poems by London School Students, 1982.

ILEA English Centre, *Our Lives*, young people's autobiographies, 1979

Levis, R., *Miracles*, London, Allen Lane, 1967. *London Through Young Eyes*, London, Dolphin, 1960.

Measham, D.C., *Fourteen*, Cambridge, Cambridge University Press, 1965.

Protherough, R. & Smith, J., *Imagine*, London, Harrap, 1974.

Searle, C., *Classroom of Resistance*, London, Writers & Readers, 1975.

Searle, C., *The World in a Classroom*, London, Writers & Readers, 1977.

Thompson, D., *Children as Poets*, London, Heinemann, 1972.

SUGGESTIONS FOR FURTHER READING

There is a mass of published information about writing. *British Books in Print* lists 250 titles with *writing* as the first major word, another 70 with *writer*(s), and 70 more with *write* or *written*. Of thousands of articles and dissertations, some of the more important have been mentioned in references to the preceding chapters, and they are not repeated here. What follows is a selective list of books and booklets likely to be currently available in libraries, (classified by major topics).

Understanding the writing process

Benton, M., *The First two Rs*, Southampton University, 1978.

Cooper, C. R. & Odell, L., *Research on Composing: Points of Departure*, Illinois, NCTE, 1978.

Elbow, P., *Writing Without Teachers*, New York, Oxford University Press, 1973.

Fairfax, J. & Moat, J., *The Way to Write*, London, Elm Tree, 1981.

Gregg, L.W. and Steinberg, E.R., *Cognitive Processes in Writing*, New Jersey, Erlsbaum, 1980.

Hartley, J., *The Psychology of Written Communication*, London, Kogan Page, 1980.

Hughes, T., *Poetry in the Making*, London, Faber & Faber 1967.

Koestler, A., *The Act of Creation*, London, Hutchinson, 1964.

Smith, F., *Writers and Writing*, London, Heinemann, 1982.

Stubbs, M., *Language and Literacy: the socio-linguistics of reading and writing*, London, Routledge & Kegan Paul, 1980.

Whitehead, F., *Creative Experiment: Writing and the Teacher*, London, Chatto & Windus, 1970.

Witkin, R.W., *The Intelligence of Feeling*, London, Heinemann, 1974.

Frameworks for considering children's writing

Bretton Language Development Unit, *A Policy for Writing 9–12*, Bretton Hall, 1981.

Britton, J. *et al.*, *The Development of Writing Abilities, 11–18*, London, Macmillan, 1975.

Dixon, J. and Stratta, L., *Achievements in Writing at 16+*, Birmingham University, 1981.

Ernig, J., *The Composing Processes of Twelfth Graders*, Illinois, NCTE, 1971.

Harpin, W., *The Second 'R'*, London, Allen & Unwin, 1976.

Martin, N. *et al.*, *Writing and Learning Across the Curriculum*, London, Ward Lock, 1967.

Moffett, J., *Teaching the Universe of Discourse*, New York, Houghton Mifflin, 1968.

Wilkinson, A. *et al.*, *Assessing Language Development*, Oxford, Oxford University Press, 1980.

Williams, J., *Learning to Write or Writing to Learn?*, Windsor, NFER, 1977.

Insights into the place of writing in school

APU, *Language Performance in Schools*, London, HMSO, 1981 onwards.

Britton, J., *Talking and Writing*, London, Methuen, 1967.

Burgess, Tony, *Understanding Children Writing*, Harmondsworth, Penguin, 1973.

Creber, J.W.P., *Lost for Words*, Harmondsworth, Penguin, 1972.

Druce, R., *The Eye of Innocence* (2nd ed.), London, ULP, 1970.

Graves, D.H., *Balance the Basics: Let them Write*, New York, Ford Foundation, 1978.

Graves, D.H., *Writing: Teachers and Children at Work*, London, Heinemann, 1983.

HMI, *Aspects of Secondary Education in England*, London, HMSO, 1979.

Holbrook, D., *English for the Rejected*, Cambridge, Cambridge University Press, 1964.

Holbrook, D., *The Secret Places*, London, Methuen, 1964.

Report of the Bullock Committee, *A Language for Life*, London, HMSO, 1975.

Lundsteen, S., *Help for the teacher of written composition: New directions in research*, Illinois, NCRE and ERIC, 1976.

Stuart, S., *Say, An experiment in learning*, London, Thomas Nelson, 1969.

Talk Workshop Group, *Becoming our own Experts*, Vauxhall Manor School, 1982.

Organizing writing within the English programme

Adams, A., *Team Teaching and the Teaching of English*, Oxford, Pergamon, 1970.

Adams, A. and Pearce, J., *Every English Teacher*, Oxford, Oxford University Press, 1974.

The Banffshire Report, *English for Mixed Ability Classes*, Grampian Regional Council, 1976.

Creber, J.W.P., *Sense and Sensitivity*, London, University of London Press, 1966.

Day, R. and Weaver, C.C., *Creative Writing in the Classroom*, an annotated bibliography, Illinois, NCTE and ERIC, 1978.

Doughty, P., Pearce, J. and Thornton, G., *Language in Use*, London, Edward Arnold, 1971.

Koch, C. and Brazil, J.M., *Strategies for Teaching the Composition Process*, Illinois, NCTE, 1978.

Larson, R.L., *Children and Writing in the Elementary School*, New York, Oxford University Press, 1975.

Mallett, M. and Newsome, B., *Talking, Writing and Learning 8–13*, London, Evans/Methuen, 1977.

Medway, P., *Finding a Language*, London, Writers and Readers, 1980.

Mills, R., *Teaching English Across the Ability Range*, London, Ward Lock, 1977.

Moffett, J., *Active Voice*, New Jersey, Boynton/Cook, 1981.

Moffett, J. and Wagner, B.J., *Student-Centered Language Arts and Reading, K13*, New York, Houghton Mifflin, 1976.

Sutton, C., *Communicating in the Classroom*, London, Hodder & Stoughton, 1981.

Thornton, G., *Teaching Writing: the development of written language skills*, London, Edward Arnold, 1980.

Torbe, M. and Protherough, R., *Classroom Encounters*, London, Ward Lock, 1976.

Whitehead, F., *The Disappearing Dais*, London, Chatto & Windus, 1966.

Initiating writing

Brownjohn, S., *Does It Have to Rhyme?*, London, Hodder & Stoughton, 1980.

Brownjohn, S., *What Rhymes with 'Secret'?*, London, Hodder & Stoughton, 1982.

Grady, L.E. and Wilcockson, D.P., *Creative Writing in Practice – A Handbook for Teachers*, London, Blackie, 1976.

Koch, K., *Wishes, Lies and Dreams*, New York, Chelsea House, 1970.

Lane, S.M. and Kemp, M., *Approach to Creative Writing in the Primary School*, London, Blackie, 1967.

Langdon, M. *Let the Children Write*, London, Longman, 1961.

Maybury, B., *Creative Writing for Juniors* (2nd ed), London, Batsford, 1981.

Maybury, B., *Writers' Workshop, techniques in creative writing*, London, Batsford, 1979.

Powell, B., *English Through Poetry Writing*, London, Heinemann, 1968.

Pym, D., *Free Writing*, London, University of London Press, 1956.

Revising and improving children's writing

Andrews, R. and Noble, J., *From Rough to Best*, London, Ward Lock, 1982.

Centre for Educational Research & Development, *The Teaching of Spelling – a Research Brief for Teachers*, Lancaster University, 1979.

Clark, M.L. and Glynn, T., *Reading and Writing for the Child with Difficulties*, Birmingham University, 1980.

Keen, John, *Teaching English: a linguistic approach*, London, Methuen, 1978.

Marcus, M., *Diagnostic Teaching of the Language Arts*, New York, John Wiley, 1977.

Peters, M.L., *Diagnostic and Remedial Spelling Manual* (rev. edn), London, Macmillan, 1979.

Shaughnessy, M.P., *Errors and Expectations*, Oxford, New

York, 1977.

Torbe, M., *Teaching Spelling*, London, Ward Lock, 1977.

Weaver, C., *Grammar for Teachers, Perspectives and Definitions*, Illinois, NCTE, 1979.

Assessing and marking children's work

APU, *Language Performance in Schools, Primary & Secondary reports*, London, HMSO, 1981 onwards.

Britton, J.N. *et al.*, *Multiple Marking of English Compositions*, London, HMSO, 1966.

Cooper, C.R. and Odell, L., *Evaluating Writing: describing, measuring, judging*, Illinois, NCTE, 1977.

Dunsbee, T. and Ford, T., *Mark My Words*, London, Ward Lock, 1980.

LATE, *Assessing Composition*, London, Blackie, 1965.

Stibbs, A., *Assessing Children's Language*, London, Ward Lock, 1979.